Nobody's Business

Nobody's Business

Paradoxes of Privacy

Alida Brill

▲
▼▼

Addison-Wesley Publishing Company, Inc.

Reading, Massachusetts   Menlo Park, California

New York   Don Mills, Ontario   Wokingham, England

Amsterdam   Bonn   Sydney   Singapore   Tokyo

Madrid   San Juan

Darrel Yates Rist, "AIDS as Apocalypse: The Deadly Costs of an Obsession," *The Nation* magazine/The Nation Company, Inc., copyright 1989.

Letters to a Young Doctor, by Richard Selzer, copyright 1982 by David Goldman and Janet Selzer, Trustees. Reprinted by permission of Simon & Schuster, Inc.

Many of the designations used by manufacturers and sellers to distinguish their products are claimed as trademarks. Where those designations appear in this book and Addison-Wesley was aware of a trademark claim, the designations have been printed in initial capital letters (e.g., Campbell).

Library of Congress Cataloging-in-Publication Data

Brill, Alida.
 Nobody's business : paradoxes of privacy / by Alida Brill.
  p. cm.
 Includes index.
 ISBN 0-201-06745-5
 1. Privacy, Right of—United States. 2. Abortion—Law and legislation—United States. 3. Artificial insemination, Human—Law and legislation—United States. 4. Medical records—Law and legislation—United States. 5. Pornography—United States.
 6. Right to die—United States. I. Title.
 KF1262.B75   1990
 342.73'0858—dc20
 [347.302858]   90-623
                                                                          CIP

Jacket design by Marge Anderson
Text design by Barbara Werden
Set in 11-point Trump Medieval by Ampersand Publisher Services, Inc., Owings Mills, MD

ABCDEFGHIJ-MW-943210
First printing, September 1990

To my parents, ALB and IHLB,
with love and admiration

Contents

Two: The Opening of the American Womb

Three: Hearts and Souls: A Privacy Metaphor

Four: Last Rights

Prologue

Paradox: Exhibiting contradictory or inexplicable aspects or qualities; an essentially self-contradictory assertion based on valid deduction from acceptable premises. Synonyms: CONTRARIETY; DILEMMA; IMPOSSIBILITY; INCONSISTENCY.

This book is about the impossibility and the dilemma of privacy—why it is, by its very nature, a confusion and how, over the course of the last years, it has become arguably the most problematic of our public issues. This is an essay about privacy in life's most intimate realms: in birth and reproductive choice; in sexual orientation; in ways of dying.

Why delve into these contradictory puzzles? Is there a use for a definitional unscrambling game, beyond the intrigue of the intellectual exercise of "compare and contrast"? I think there is. The terrain of privacy is where many of our ethical and public policy decisions will be made in the next decade and on into the next century. If we are not to wake up too late to find our civility and integrity as a people diminished, we must face up, honestly and courageously, to the privacy issues raised, especially in these most intimate domains.

A tree house is marked in an almost illegible childhood scrawl: "Clubhouse—Keep Out—This Means You." This is the private world of children under ten. The childhood ritual of hiding places, secret spots safe from the grown-ups, suggests how deeply embedded the notion of privacy is in our communal psyche. It is our custom to claim areas of our lives as private—off-limits to intruders, snooping eyes and ears. We draw the line between the self and the world pretty early on. Once it is drawn, most of us protect that line fiercely. From this early age many of us learn to sound the warning "nobody's business." We mean by this, "Stand clear, no prying, because I am entitled to keep some information and parts of my life to myself."

Louis Brandeis wrote a phrase that has become, for many, a privacy watchword. He said that privacy was the "right most valued by civilized people," that it was "the right to be let alone." These words continue to resonate. We believe it an inherent, perhaps an inviolable, right to define for ourselves what can be known or revealed, and to whom, and to choose what we want to hide, or to veil, from public scrutiny.

In our public battles to extend privacy, however, we have transformed the common sense of privacy into "everybody's business" in order to make it, legally and officially, nobody's business once again. Have we as a society become hopelessly mired in a series of contradictions and confusions? An insightful Martian journalist visiting our planet might well ask us to explain our odd behavior.

How do we reconcile asking for more secrecy and more privacy while using the most public of legal devices and other national forums?

The line between the public and the private is a fuzzy boundary, and it has become even more blurred in the last twenty-five years or so. Controversies about public versus private are newsworthy stories; we find them on the front pages of our newspapers and on our television news programs. Although our custom from childhood forward may be to guard certain things from others, our tradition of reform is public, litigious, and political. As a people we have learned to protect our rights through activism, social movement, litigation, legislation.

These are not ineffective methods for expanding liberty. Sometimes, however, this public commitment for the expansion of liberty crashes up against the walls we have built to protect our privacy. Yet we continue to believe that it is our right to claim areas of our lives as off-limits. These acts are puzzling and not always efficacious to our ends.

The classical citizen of Athens knew that there was a difference between the public and the private—and resolved any possibility of a paradox by disavowing the worth of the private life. The public life was the only recognized life—and perhaps this omission protected the salon from the invasion of anti-gay or anti-libation zealots. But we are not in classical Athens; indeed, we are not in early constitutional America. What needs to be guarded today far exceeds our collective understanding and imagination. There are those who claim that what we want to keep private will harm the community at large—that revealing our deepest secrets may be deemed to be in the public interest.

Privacy's continuation demands answers to tough questions: how much individual privacy are you willing to give up to increase the likelihood of a safer society, of a healthier society, of a less mortal society? But these are meaningless questions, unless asked in the first person. That is, we must confront ourselves and ask not how much of our neighbor's privacy we are willing to barter away for the public good but how much of our own privacy we are willing to give up.

While our constitutional founders could not have envisioned the world we now live in with much precision, it is well to remember that nowhere in the document did they include the phrase "right to privacy." Although they spelled out the government's restrictions in matters of search and seizure, and laid the groundwork for a myriad of privacy decisions and guarantees, they never uttered the word *privacy* nor did they come close to graphically demarcating the line between the public and the private.

What should and should not be private has become the stuff of bitter legal and political controversy. All of democratic life is a trade-off; we are always engaged in a balancing act of freedom versus control. It is in the area of privacy, however, that the question "at what cost freedom/at what loss control" becomes both troubling and contradictory.

A Key, A Lock, A Door.

Where does it begin, this seemingly instinctive but obviously culture-bound need for secrecy—this demand that a portion of our lives be regarded as private? It is far beyond the scope of this essay to attempt to isolate the psychological origins of privacy in the American psyche, but what can be said is that it appears to be present from almost the beginning, and that it is, even in its crudest and earliest forms, the desire or the attempt to be protected from invasion, control, intrusion, exposure.

What this implies is that, from the beginning, privacy is dependent on the behavior of others, whether it be the behavior of other family members, the society, the courts, our body of laws, the norms of a neighborhood, or the personal code of ethics of a journalist. Privacy is granted to an individual only when others agree to honor that privacy, be it by compliance with the law or by community custom. However fiercely we protect our emotional or actual borders, intrusion cannot be held off if someone is interested in breaking through and is ultimately successful in that endeavor.

If you live or work in New York City and rush through Grand Central Terminal early in the morning at the start of your workday, you will see many of the homeless engaging in their morning ablutions. As your gaze finds them, you choose, in that very moment, to grant them privacy or to observe them—openly or coyly. Their privacy is in your hands moment to moment, day after day.

Structures help us shut the world out; property, individual shelter, helps us keep our secrets. Privacy may guard a mysterious life and may be the stuff of gossip, romance, and intrigue, or privacy may simply afford the plain old comfortable "peace and quiet." Whatever the style or the reason, privacy is unmistakably the stuff of the "landed gentry." I suspect that the men in Grand Central Terminal, who have to turn their backs as they change their trousers, would agree. Your kind and good manners, or as Tennessee Williams termed it "the kindness of strangers," are the doors they rely on as they attempt to achieve the thinnest slice of a private life.

In our homes we hide our sorrows, our troubles, our joys, our sensual afternoons. All of these amenities come with the key, the lock, the door, the domicile, the common castle of humankind—the home. Perhaps the reason that the Soviet citizen has such a translation problem with the word *privacy* has as much to do with the spatial problems as political ideology. With three generations often residing in a tiny apartment, what we would recognize as elementary privacy does not often survive.

We do not carry privacy in our backpacks beyond our hiding places. Children discover this when they leave their secret clubhouses and adolescent diaries behind.

Privacy is granted to you by others, by their decency, by their understanding, by their compassionate behavior, by the laws of the land. It exists only when others let you have it—privacy is an accorded right.

Books have always begun in people's heads before the first words go from the pen onto the paper. Now, before the screen of the personal computer beeps, the soul stirs with our experiences suggesting a personal view of how the world seems to be ordered. Writers point to "that day when. . . . " Virginia Woolf, crossing the great yard at the great university in England, musing about the variety of places and libraries barred to women, began in that moment what was to become *A Room of One's Own*. Susan Sontag's own bout with cancer led to the writing of *Illness as Metaphor*. Sometimes we write when something profoundly moving or disturbing happens to us.

While I have written a good bit about civil liberties in general, my interest in the complexity and impossibility of privacy began with an especially frightening bout with a chronic, and sometimes debilitating, illness. I was in and out of the hospital enough times to elicit concern among my friends and doctors, and I proved to be an interesting enough case to keep many young residents and interns far too stimulated about its course. Because I was a patient in a major teaching hospital, it was commonplace for residents and interns to come along on rounds while I was displayed and openly discussed. Lying in hospital rooms day after day, I felt stripped of any dignity—a rather typical complaint of the sick and hospitalized person, but I also found myself losing privacy in unanticipated ways.

Friends and the various medical staff all learned more about me than I might have elected that they know. I felt an ebbing away of any structure that would allow me to guard or keep anything to myself. This book, then, is really a result of my own journey into a world where I felt I could protect little of myself and where I first began to think about the puzzles of personal privacy.

The feeling of exposure, of having been robbed of my intimate self, the fear about who might decide things about my life, made me ponder the meaning and the fragility of privacy in our lives. Privacy and vulnerability are not compatible partners. The more vulnerable you are, the less likely it is that you will feel empowered or enabled to protect your privacy.

Think about those times when it would be most preferable to protect your privacy, and they largely suggest times when one is at a weak point physically or emotionally—when you want to have an abortion; when your sexuality challenges a societal taboo; when you or a family member are ill, perhaps dying; when you are homeless and poor; when you are embroiled in a nasty custody battle with your former spouse.

The list is virtually endless. These are times when one feels or is in fact either powerless or beleaguered. Yet these are the times when privacy is most cherished. Without power, without property, without resources and lots of courage, invasions of privacy are all the more possible, and the infringements on it are thus all the more painful.

These are actual, not philosophical, questions and events that plague us as Americans committed to freedom, equality, and individual liberty. They plague us because liberty, freedom, and equality, to our despair, are in a kind of perpetual juggling act with one another, forcing us to confront the inequities of our system by race, class, gender, and income. Such balancing acts remind us that whatever the guarantees of the Constitution, as written, or as interpreted by judicial opinion, our society is one where the freedom on which it is based allows very divergent, indeed irreconcilable, positions to endure, with proponents on each side claiming legitimacy under the creed of American democracy.

Does the phrase "nobody's business" belong to a more innocent time—a time when we understood that minding your own business was half the bargain? The other half required at least a tacit understanding that conformity brought the protections of privacy and that nonconformity probably risked "blowing your cover." The key, the lock, the door, metaphorically and actually, were the tools that controlled privacy in a simpler time. Privacy may still be considered and fought for as an individual liberty, but as individuals acting alone we can no longer control and safeguard our privacy. Technology and lifestyles have made privacy protection a very different endeavor. At the same time, the kinds of privacy infringements that are possible inside individual lives have moved from a class of somewhat benign nuisances to crippling mandates and restrictions.

Privacy is a vast and complex country, a land of perplexity; it is a troublesome terrain, characterized by paradox. This book is, I trust, a bit of a chart through the maze, through the trade-offs, the sacrifices, the confusions. It strikes me that the graphic representation that applies in privacy is really that of a map, or the lack of one—we do not have a map to guide.

Friends of mine are sailing enthusiasts; they like to sail the challenging waters of Maine. One summer day we were sailing back to Camden harbor, and my friends let out a scream as they saw a motorboat zipping across the waters of the harbor and heading out to sea. One of them covered his eyes and said, "Oh my God." I saw nothing wrong; they then explained that the course the motorboat had chosen was filled with sandbars, rock croppings, and the like. "They must not have a harbor map . . . who would set out to sea without a navigation map?" my friend asked.

High seas and the mermaids saved the motorboat from disaster that day. As a society we have set out on very dangerous waters without a navigation map. We have learned, and are still learning, that the mermaids and the tides have not always been there to protect us. Increasingly, we are understanding that we have to start plotting our soundings in this important harbor of privacy, in order to chart a course as a nation—and that we must do so with wisdom, tolerance, compassion, and a sense of urgency.

Alida Brill
East Hampton, New York
March 1990

Part One

Family Secrets

Secrets, Gossip, Mystery

I was about ten years old when it became apparent to me that people had secrets, families had secrets, and I too had secrets. The business of guarding those secrets was fascinating to me then and has remained so throughout my life. I was a child in the 1950s, and it was largely expected that one kept quiet about these family secrets. "Talking out of school" could bring a strong reprimand from a parent or other adult. One friend's mother drank too much, another's father took it on the lam, to pursue the fairer sex or to gamble. Whatever the neighborhood tales, it was likely they would remain in that whispered form of communication—gossip.

Saul Bellow, a product of his time, once said that "a woman without secrets is hardly a woman at all." Women of my mother's generation and of earlier generations were ill at ease discussing openly the details of their pregnancies. Even the event of a miscarriage was something kept

3

under wraps. I recall a neighbor's miscarriage as a shadowy thing, a quiet event guarded by her family and friends.

Abortion, as a completely illegal action, was something whispered about, something hidden. For those who could obtain the expensive, elusive, somewhat safe abortion, there were disappearances for a few weeks, unexplained trips to Europe, to Mexico. For those who could not afford it or had no access, babies were given up for adoption, young girls sent off to "homes for unwed mothers." Women who panicked tried do-it-yourself abortions, often with disastrous and tragic results, or found themselves butchered by abortion "practitioners."

"Jane Roe" Gives Birth to a Paradox

All of this changed in 1973 when a young woman named Norma McCorvey became the "Jane Roe" of the historic landmark case *Roe v. Wade.* Since the Brandeis days of the "right to be let alone," privacy has evolved from a passive, to an active, right. People no longer want to sit around basking in the quiet comfort of their right to be let alone and the solitude it might bring them. People want and need to do something in this privacy. One of the primary things many women want to be able to do in this active realm of privacy is to choose to have an abortion.

The abortion decision of the U.S. Supreme Court in 1973 gave women the right to choose to terminate a pregnancy by abortion, and they placed that right inside the domain of privacy. We might say that women gave up their secrets in order to gain their privacy. It would be wrong, however, to tell the American story of abortion in terms of absolute victory, followed by beginning loss, and perhaps final defeat. In fact, the American saga after *Roe* is of an immediate escalation of women's rights, followed fairly swiftly by a continued and unwavering curtailment and limitation of those rights.

In essence, the Court's decision said that a pregnant woman had a right to privacy by virtue of her pregnancy and not by virtue of her citizenship. A kind of conditional privacy "for women only."

While there is no *direct* constitutional reference to privacy, its sanctity has long been recognized by the Supreme Court, which has held that any number of individual actions should be protected from government intrusion, invasion, and restriction. Of its privacy decisions, however, undoubtedly the most controversial and far-reaching has been the 1973 *Roe v. Wade* decision.*

---

* The Supreme Court's history of substantive constitutional privacy really begins in 1965 with the *Griswold v. Connecticut* case. The state of Connecticut had an ancient and little-used statute prohibiting the use of contraceptives and an additional statute provision that made "aiding or abetting" their use a crime. These laws were invoked to keep a Planned Parenthood birth control clinic from opening in New Haven, Connecticut. The Supreme Court, in a 7 to 2 decision, reversed the conviction against the directors of Planned Parenthood. Justice Douglas in his opinion for the Court concluded that "a relationship lying within the zone of privacy [is] a right older than the Bill of Rights," thus suggesting that, at least in the view of Justice Douglas, the right to privacy in a sense superseded and outdated the formal coda of the Constitution.

Two Supreme Court justices dissented in the *Roe* decision. They were Rehnquist and White. Justice Blackmun wrote the Court's opinion, which said that the "right of privacy is broad enough to encompass a woman's decision whether or not to terminate her pregnancy." However, the Court concluded that abortion "is not unqualified and must be considered against important state interests in regulation."

Prevailing legal doctrine in privacy decisions derives its doctrinal source from the Due Process Clause of the Fourteenth Amendment—that is, those cases involving what Gary Bostwick has called the "zone of intimate decision" as opposed to the questions of privacy coming under the Search and Seizure clauses of the Fourth Amendment. On the face of it, then, privacy seems to belong to the larger issues of procedural fairness—"not to be deprived of life, liberty or property . . . without due process of law."

The Struggle for Control

The "important state interests in regulation" were the health interests that might be promoted by regulation of procedures after the first trimester (the first three months of pregnancy) and the potentiality of human life (in simple language that is the provision the Court originally made for the protection of "fetus viability"). The statement regarding life, although seemingly benign, has been the focus for much of the battle to maintain abortion rights. In reality, however, due to the *Roe* decision, there was virtually no prohibition on abortion prior to approximately the last three months of a pregnancy until the *Webster* decision in 1989.

Nonetheless, these qualified guarantees, opening the opportunity for some restrictions, foreshadow much of what has happened in the strategy of right-to-life groups. Abortion remains the most dramatic and troubled of the Court's constitutional extensions of privacy. Perhaps no other liberty is as volatile as the right to choose to terminate a pregnancy. Abortion has been hotly debated and threatened; the Reagan years witnessed nearly daily challenges. The *Webster* decision in the summer of 1989 was one outcome of these challenges.

The Reagan administration was unyielding and unwavering in its attacks on the right to choose an abortion. Its strategy was threefold: limit access; limit information; attempt to overturn *Roe*.

The concerted and well-financed effort of the right-to-life groups has been tremendously aided by the support of "affinity" groups in the New Right and in the religious Fundamentalist Right. There have been incidents of domestic terrorism where abortion clinics and Planned Parenthood offices have been bombed and their staff threatened. Operation Rescue has used the nonviolent strategies of the civil rights movement to close down or hamper women's health clinics and clog the court system with protest arrests.

This private decision on the part of a woman has ⟩

become not only the content of the hottest and most bitter of public and legal debates and challenges but a most helpful political tool as well. What used to be a family's secret, or a woman's hidden agony, is now in the open and part of political campaign rhetoric.

Opposition to abortion has become the rallying point for American conservatives and members of the New Right. It is now commonplace for some candidates and incumbents to strongly, or even primarily, identify themselves as pro-life or right-to-life candidates. Some have done so without much reference to other parts of their ideological framework. Others have used as the rationale for their candidacy the solemn pledge to eliminate abortion from the land, as though this alone should qualify a person for elected office. As part of his acceptance speech at the Republican National Convention in the summer of 1988, George Bush stated, from the convention podium, his intention to remove abortion from the land.

In the 1960s, student reformers and activists often said that "the personal is political" in an attempt to draw attention to individual actions as important aspects of social change. Now the world has changed in such a way that the personal of abortion has become the political of the Fundamentalist New Right and their allies. In short, what Justice Blackmun attempted to protect under a new kind of privacy guarantee of the U.S. Constitution has been violently attacked in that most public of arenas as something immoral and reprehensible—and above all, seemingly everybody's business, except the pregnant woman's. Yet both the reality and the rhetoric of the *Roe* decision dictate much of our current notion of privacy. In short, *Roe* forever altered the face of privacy—what we can expect, how we define privacy, and how far its parameters might extend.

"Doctor Doesn't Always Know Best"— *The Flaw of* Roe

Judicial reasoning about privacy often includes the phrase "the legitimate expectation of privacy." There are few areas of a woman's life where this expectation, on the face of it, would seem more legitimate. The Court indeed did recognize the validity of privacy in this context. Yet privacy was also forever confused in the *Roe* decision because privacy was also made public in some basic and fundamental way. The complicating language of *Roe* is this: by stating that this very private decision should occur between a woman and her doctor, an irreconcilable conflict was put into place. The Court did not say "between a woman and her conscience or her God, with some advice from her doctor"; nor did the Court say "between a woman and the father of her child, if she so chooses." The Court said, instead, "between a woman and her doctor."

Even if the reality of abortion, prior to the *Webster* decision, had little to do with a doctor's actual opinion, and women routinely have made abortion decisions on their own, the language and the precedent of *Roe* set up a fundamental contradiction that made both women and privacy vulnerable. The right-to-life suits against doctors performing abortions indicate the public nature of their profession and their legal roles in the abortion decisions of their patients. The anti-abortion doctors who help file fetal-neglect suits against women additionally underline the public and confounding aspects of the *Roe v. Wade* language.

If we put aside for the moment the time-honored notion of the confidential nature of the doctor-patient relationship and the precedent of including the physician in such cases, we can better consider the inherently public nature of this newly crafted privacy right. A doctor is not yourself, not your sister, not your lover, not your soul, and not your husband. A doctor is usually someone outside the family and unrelated to you. Perhaps in a nostalgic moment we romantically characterize the doctor as an adopted additional family member, not unlike the lovable country doc, or Marcus Welby, M.D., of television fame. However, a doctor, although he or she may or may not be a stranger to the woman involved, is in a public, not a familial, role with regard to the pregnant woman. Increasingly in the years since *Roe* we have seen women's rights challenged by the medical profession.

There was probably little else Justice Blackmun could have done in 1973 to construct an opinion that would have gotten by the majority of the Court. The final outcome was not Justice Blackmun's first attempt at the opinion that became the majority decision. While my remarks are an exegesis of *Roe*, they are not intended to criticize the intent of the justices who fought for the right of abortion.

They are instead consideration of that solemn power of language, as it relates especially to the definition and action of privacy in our lives, particularly as it is enforced and codified. The rhetorician Richard Weaver said that "language is sermonic"—its impact often far surpasses the author's moment of inspiration. The power of language, as well as its fragility and imprecise nature, often come back to influence and change meaning, direction, outcome.

The First Erosion: No Public Funds

Whether one argues that the *Roe* guarantee is weak or strong, the Supreme Court has consistently restricted the public funding of abortions. Although it may seem logical to deny the public funding of such a private decision, right to this kind of privacy is essentially denied to those who cannot buy it. (The notable cases are in 1977, *Maher v. Roe*, 432 U.S. 464, and in 1980, *Harris v. McRae*, 448, U.S. 297.)

In the cases where the Court has held that state and federal government is constitutionally entitled to exclude abortions from comprehensive medical programs providing care to indigents and the poor, it has all but prohibited certain women's use of that right. The significant impact those decisions have on a large segment of the female population essentially forbids them to exercise the abortion option.

Both *Maher* and *Harris* foreclosed the privacy option to many in all but a theoretical manner. Every woman may have had the right to an abortion, but the right to exercise it was now limited to those with a fat checkbook. Paul Bender sees these access problems as a further indication of the quintessentially "middle-class" approach to privacy rights. Bender contends that what the funding cases show is "that the Court is satisfied, at least at present, to tolerate a situation where constitutional privacy rights are available in theory to everyone, but are in fact available only to the more affluent members of society."

In *Maher*, a Connecticut restriction on payments of state Medicaid benefits for abortions was upheld by the Supreme Court, which said that the state was under no obligation to treat abortion and childbirth equally. In many ways consistent with its original reasoning, the Court held that "no obstacles were placed in the pregnant woman's path to an abortion [with such a restriction]."

In other words, the Court reasoned that the state of Connecticut simply found childbirth a more attractive alternative than abortion. Thus, if a woman's poverty kept her from an abortion, the result could not be seen as an outcome or a result of the Connecticut restriction. The Court therefore held that the state was not interfering with a protected activity but was encouraging another activity (motherhood) considered to be more in the public interest. In the *Harris* case the Court continued its support of the prohibition of federal funds, in this case even when medically necessary. Justice Stewart said that these cases did not impinge on the right recognized in *Roe* because

> ... it simply does not follow that a woman's freedom of choice carries with it a constitutional entitlement to the financial resources to avail herself of the full range of protected choices ... [T]he fact remains that the Hyde Amendment* leaves an indigent woman with at least the same range of choice in deciding whether to obtain a medically necessary abortion as she would have had if Congress had chosen to subsidize no health care costs at all.

The *Thornburgh* Case:
Roe Slides Further

In June 1986 the Supreme Court significantly weakened the guarantees of *Roe* and put in place the beginning foundation for fetal rights. The case began as *Thornburgh*

---

*The exact language of the Hyde Amendment reads: "None of the funds contained in this Act shall be used to perform abortions except where the life of the mother would be endangered if the fetus were carried to term" (Labor Appropriations Act of 1977, HR 14232). In fact, the only exceptions provided by the Hyde Amendment involve an abortion for a woman whose life is actually threatened or for a victim of rape or incest.

v. American College of Obstetricians and Gynecologists.
The Court did vote to uphold the *Roe* decision, but it was
a very divided decision (5 to 4). The Pennsylvania state
law in question was judged to deter abortion in some instances and to risk maternal life for fetal life in others.

The *New York Times* lead article on June 12, 1986,
headlined the decision in the following way:

> JUSTICES UPHOLD ABORTION RIGHTS BY NARROW VOTE.
> COURT IS DEEPLY DIVIDED.
> BURGER SHIFT RAISES POSSIBILITY OF REVERSAL OF
> POSITION IF MEMBERSHIP CHANGES.

Dateline: Washington June 11, 1986

A deeply divided Supreme Court today reaffirmed its
landmark 1973 decision establishing a constitutional
right to abortion which the Reagan Administration had
urged it to abandon.

Justice Blackmun reasserted his understanding of the
inherent privacy of the abortion decision and stated:

The states are not free under the guise of protecting
maternal health or potential life to intimidate women
into continuing pregnancies.

Acknowledging profound moral and spiritual debate
around the reality of abortion, he nevertheless concluded:

14

[that the Constitution] embodies a promise that a certain private sphere will be kept largely beyond the reach
of government.

Although Justice Burger had been in agreement with
the language of *Roe* and with the right to abortion that it
set up, he shifted his allegiance in this decision, thus un-
alterably setting the stage for the 1989 limitations which
would come with the *Webster* decision. Burger felt that
Roe needed to be reexamined and that the post-*Roe* years
had failed to see much, if any, regulation of late-term
abortions. For Burger the *Roe* decision had spawned the
era of "abortion on demand."

The Pennsylvania law involved in this case was known
as the 1982 Pennsylvania Abortion Control Act, which
had, among other provisions, those requiring that women
be provided with detailed information on the risks of
abortion and on its alternatives. It also required the presence of two doctors in late-term abortions and said abortions must be performed in such a way that they would
produce live births of the fetuses unless that would pose
"significantly greater risk" to the women.

Justice White, who was one of the original dissenters
in 1973, said that even if he had agreed with *Roe*, the
Pennsylvania law was still in keeping with the spirit and
the intention of regulating late abortions, and preserving
fetus viability. Justice O'Connor, the Court's only
woman, dissented from the majority opinion, which
favored the continuation of *Roe's* principles.

She wrote:

This Court's abortion decisions have already worked a major distortion in the Court's constitutional jurisprudence. Today's decision goes further, and makes it painfully clear that no legal rule or doctrine is safe from ad hoc nullification by this Court when an occasion for its application arises in a case involving state regulation of abortion.

It was Justice John Paul Stevens who perhaps most concisely expressed the public/private dichotomy when he said:

It is far better to permit some individuals to make incorrect decisions than to deny all individuals the right to make decisions that have a profound effect upon their destiny.

The *Thornburgh* case illustrates perfectly the paradoxical muddle of contemporary privacy. This case was filed in its original lawsuit by a group of doctors who wanted to strike down the Pennsylvania law; the Reagan forces, in their anti-abortion zeal, had Solicitor General Charles Fried file a brief for the Reagan administration as a "friend of the Court." In that brief he urged the Court to overrule its 1973 decision, leaving states free to do as they chose with the right to abortion.

It was the administration's attempt to get the Court to strike down its own prior decision that activated so much fundraising and support on both sides of the issue. Anti-abortion advocates hailed the decision as hopeful because of the narrow margin, and most important, because of Burger's dramatic shift, calling the attention away from the question of privacy and focusing instead on the need for regulation. Abortion rights groups correctly hailed the defeat of the administration's anti-abortion activism as a very important victory.

What Is a Woman—
Private Citizen or Pregnant Subject?

The 1986 *Thornburgh* decision highlighted the conflicts originated in *Roe*—was it about the right of privacy or the right to have an abortion?

What happened in *Thornburgh*, it seems to me, is that the privacy legitimacy of *Roe* was exposed in a most complicated and, in many ways, perverse manner. Blackmun said in 1986 what he was not prepared to say in 1973: that essentially nothing matters more than the privacy of the woman—the sanctity of her womb and the inescapable personal or intimate nature of that decision. Here we see little of the previous lip service to medical opinion or to fetus viability. We see instead the father of pro-choice saying that this is what *Roe* was always about: the privacy of a woman to choose this desperately sad, totally personal action.

Burger, in a reversal, says: I recall *Roe* differently. It was not about an unlimited broad-based kind of privacy that could be applied without concern universally by any and all pregnant women so desiring, it was about a quite limited right, under some conditions, and not on the massive scale we now have. Privacy, in the Burger view, was secondary to a number of things. What the 1986 reaffirmation of *Roe* through *Thornburgh* did was to underline dramatically the precariously dangerous business of placing abortion under a rubric exclusively defined by privacy.

It should be noted that the Supreme Court, in 1925 in a case entitled *Pierce v. Society of Sisters*, recognized the home and family as the sphere protected from government intrusion and intervention. It is this traditional definition of the family that some legal experts, such as Susan Estrich and Virginia Kerr, suggest accounts for the traditionality present in *Roe*. Thus the language of *Roe* must be seen in the context of this history. Justice Blackmun's remarks in *Thornburgh*, then, should be seen as more than a rhetorical device and instead as actual movement away from the family sphere of protected privacy for women and into the world of public citizen protected in her private actions.

Extending privacy, Blackmun essentially backpedaled the state interest in fetal life potentiality and returned the woman to the forefront. Burger, on the other hand, retreated from the notion of privacy as the ultimate right. He suggested instead a total reexamination of *Roe*, affirming its nature as abortion-based and abortion limited, and *not privacy controlled*.

By stating that the basic right to privacy must extend equally to women as it does to men, it would appear that Blackmun was trying to move women, if ever so carefully, into a protection of their privacy based also on their citizenship and not exclusively on the condition of their pregnancy. Having built a nifty little house out of the Fourteenth Amendment, he perhaps began to see that the roof extended beyond the rooms of the house and in 1986 began to build the equality rooms underneath the constitutional roof. This may be an apt metaphor, since the 1989 *Webster* decision would see Justice Scalia, a violent enemy of abortion, use the house-of-the-law metaphor not as a builder but as part of its demolition crew.

The Secrets of Girlhood: Now Rated "X"

As a teenager, I remember the ritual of my first diary. For all of my friends, the little locked book was one of our most valued and precious possessions. My gang of pals and I would write in our diaries regularly, bury them in our drawer, usually our underwear drawer, and then check often to be sure they had not been tampered with by snooping siblings or, God forbid, invaded by the dread eyes of our parents! Girls today have more to protect than their diaries; the sexual revolution is perhaps most obvious in the lives of teenagers. Gone are the innocent days of peeking up skirts, heavy petting in the drive-in movie, or the furtive secret and forbidden lovemaking of the past. Today's teenagers live with the kind of sexual intensity previously reserved for one's college years and beyond. The vast number of teenage pregnancies (now more than a million a year) and the soaring rate of abortions performed on young women under the age of eighteen illustrate most vividly this loss of innocence. Most of us openly acknowledge that the young, and in some cases *the very young*, have full sexual lives and experiences.

We used to protect our daughters within the family unit; now some girls seek protection from their parents outside the family unit. The obligation of a doctor to inform the parents of a minor about a proposed abortion remains one of the murkiest and most complicated parts of the abortion issue. Known originally as the "squeal rule," it has come more recently to be known by its legal requirement, the "notification rule."

Many say that privacy is something that must be earned with years and with experience—that the exercise of privacy by one's children interferes in their raising and may conflict with parents' morals and values. The problem is that at this phase in our society's mores, young girls engage in womanly sexual activities, producing the need to take very grown-up, autonomous steps. A 1981 Supreme Court case rather clearly undermined a young woman's right to privacy. In that case (*Matheson*, 450 U.S. 298 [1981]), the Court found it proper for a family to know about an adolescent's sexual life. It said that a Utah law that required parental notification when the girl was living with and supported by her parents promoted the integrity of family life. Other cases have added to this precedent.

Although the courts seem reluctant to exclude *Roe*

completely from applying to girls, they tend to sidestep privacy in their decisions. What seems to have happened in both lower courts and the highest court is that girls have a right to an abortion but not its attendant right to privacy. In other words, for a girl to activate the privacy guarantee underpinning *Roe*, she must first cancel it by revealing or exposing the fact of her pregnancy. Because most girls are dependent on their parents in virtually all major ways, notification laws essentially invade the entirety of the *Roe* premise by placing the decision in the hands of the parents. The ability to bypass parental disapproval and obtain a judicial court order allowing abortion even if the parents refuse does exist in some states. The American Civil Liberties Union believes these laws interfere with liberty and contend they are designed for parental control, not parental help. This is complicated terrain because on the one hand the notion of children undergoing surgical procedures without parental consent is virtually unknown. Yet investing parents with veto powers over their daughters' abortions essentially denies freedom of choice to young women. And with the notification rule the girl with a difficult family situation (such as violence, abuse, alcohol, or drugs) has little recourse short of the judicial court order or seeking an abortion in a state with more lenient laws. In the more tragic cases, girls frightened by their parents have taken desperate measures—some leading to their deaths.

In June of 1990, the Court upheld an Ohio law requiring girls under the age of 18 to notify one parent or to obtain a judge's permission to have an abortion. The vote was 6 to 3. In the same day, the Court held that a Minnesota law requiring notification of both parents was constitutional, because that state provides the option of a judicial hearing. The vote in this case was 5 to 4. (*Ohio v. Akron Center for Reproductive Health* and *Hodgson v. Minnesota.*

Some state courts have held for girls, saying that they are mature enough to decide whether they want pregnancy or abortion. Minors have been granted the right to privacy in their school possessions. An interesting contrast to that is a case called *New Jersey v. TLO*, but this case was decided under a much less complicated privacy umbrella—the search and seizure provisions of the Fourth Amendment. Protecting the privacy of your possessions in some real way belongs to a simpler time and is more easily guarded than questions of bodily privacy. Beneath the judicial wanderings and reasonings lies the crux of the issue. At what age does a person possess privacy entitlements, and over what issues? In other words, is the expectation and realization of privacy embedded in the individual acts of the person, or in the person's chronological age?

From Roe *To Woe*

April 1989. The spring of great feminist and civil libertarian anxiety. The March on Washington for Women's Equality and Women's Lives. It is, in reality, a massive show of support for pro-choice abortion rights. Generations of women march together—grandmothers, mothers, daughters, granddaughters, as well as fathers, sons, lovers, supporters. Mothers of the women's rights movement, including Betty Friedan, march, Friedan with her own daughter, a physician, the grandchild carried in an infant backpack.

Everywhere on the march route young women marched with placards that stated "Supreme Court Justices: Keep Your Laws Off My Body." Women in their forties and older carried signs with coat hangers attached, saying "Never Again"—a stark symbol and reminder of the back-alley style abortions prior to its legalization sixteen years before. An enormous coat hanger made of white wire,

23

with blood-red crepe paper streaming from its hook, made its way along the parade route—waving a bit in the wind, unsteady because of its size. Its effect was chilling.

Feminists and friends of a woman's right to choose feared a virtual reversal of the historic *Roe* decision, but the strength of the numbers on April 9, 1989, and the determination of the crowd betrayed the fears and the unlucky numbers on the Court (a crowd whose numbers were estimated at a low of 300,000 to a high of 500,000).

Before the Supreme Court was a case that could remove or restrict severely the right to choice. The case, beginning in Missouri, was known in the vernacular of both the right-to-life and right-to-choose groups as simply *Webster*, for the name of the attorney general of Missouri who brought the case forward on behalf of the state. Missouri was determined to end abortion within its borders if it could possibly get away with it. This was the Court's chance to attack the right to abortion profoundly and directly, and the first major abortion rights decision before the Court since the full complement of Reagan-appointed justices.

* * *

> For today, at least, the law of abortion stands undisturbed. For today, the women of this nation still retain the liberty to control their destinies. But the signs are evident and very ominous, and a chill wind blows. I dissent.
>
> *Justice Harry A. Blackmun (1989)*

That summer the cold wind did indeed blow. In a 5 to 4 plurality opinion, the Supreme Court severely restricted the scope of *Roe* in its *Webster* ruling.

The *Webster* decision did two things—that is, it did two significantly bad things to women and, ultimately, to the larger society:

1. Access to public facilities for abortion was essentially denied to women, thereby hampering the exercise of one's civil rights.

2. The Court closed its eyes to the import of the terrible mixing of theology (i.e., religion) with a supposed constitutional right.

This one decision is so frightening because it represents both a diminution in the civil rights gains of the last decades and because it threatens to harm our original (colonial) prohibition against any establishment of a particular religious conviction as a part of our laws or constitutional guarantees.

*Conception, the Court,
and St. Thomas Aquinas*

Five justices of the Supreme Court (Chief Justice Rehnquist and Justices White, O'Connor, Scalia, and Kennedy) decided that it was fine to let the premise of the preamble of the Missouri Statute stand without debate. This is particularly troubling because it is not a passive preamble. It states that "the life of each human being begins at conception ... and that unborn children have protectable interests in life, health and well-being ... and that all state laws be interpreted to provide *unborn children* with the same rights enjoyed by *other persons*, subject to the federal Constitution and this Court's precedents" (from the *Webster* decision) (my emphasis).

Despite the scientific understanding to the contrary that "pregnancy begins not with conception, but with implantation," each of these justices suggests that the Missouri Statute's preamble about the beginning of life does not in and of itself constitute a constitutional violation. They contend it is simply the state's expression of a *preferred value*. That value judgment is that the option of motherhood is more important to the interests of the state than the option of abortion. Condoning a state's interest in motherhood over abortion is not new terrain for the Court; it has previously indicated the right of the state to opt for motherhood in its justification and rationale for the curtailment of federal aid and state funds for abortions.

However, the Missouri preamble, although perhaps not such a thundering legal problem at the moment, is more than the mild value judgment those justices would have us believe it is. Instead it is the *expressed theological* tenet of more than a few Christian sects. In fact, the amici brief filed by the Lutheran Church of the Missouri Synod et al. noted that the view that life begins at conception is a long-held and deeply cherished religious belief. Here we are confronted with those who see religion not as an intimate, faithful, private interaction with a divine being but as an ideological framework that mandates certain behaviors in our communal public life.

Justice Stevens's eloquent dissent is of note here. He states that to accept into the Court's record the Missouri preamble's notion that life begins at conception is, ipso facto, to violate the Establishment Clause of the Constitution, which demands the separation of church and state. Justice Stevens reminds us of the teachings of St. Thomas Aquinas, the thirteenth-century theologian who held that the soul entered the female fetus eighty days after conception, while the male fetus received its soul forty days after conception. This precept, for a long time held as a tenet by the Catholic church, thus signified the beginning of life. Using this conceit to show the fallacy of the plurality's reasoning, Justice Stevens says:

> If the views of St. Thomas were held as widely today as they were in the Middle Ages, and if a state legislature were to enact a statute prefaced with a "finding" that female life begins 80 days after conception and male life begins 40 days after conception, I have no doubt that this Court would promptly conclude that such an endorsement of a particular religious tenet is violative of the Establishment Clause.
>
> ... The preamble to the Missouri statute endorses the theological position that there is the same secular interest in preserving the life of a fetus during the first 40 or 80 days of pregnancy as there is after viability—

27

indeed after the time when the fetus has become a "person" with legal right protected by the Constitution ... I believe Missouri has the burden of identifying the secular interests that differentiate the first 40 days of pregnancy from the period immediately before or after fertilization when, as *Griswold* and related cases establish, the Constitution allows the use of contraceptive procedures to prevent potential life from developing into full personhood.

As a secular matter, there is an obvious difference between the state interest in protecting the freshly fertilized egg and the state interest in protecting a 9-month-gestated, fully sentient fetus on the eve of birth.

The Search for Fetal Viability

Interestingly, and perhaps ultimately beneficial to women, the *Webster* decision largely stays away from an argument on the merits of personal privacy. Instead, the trimester approach of *Roe* is attacked. This decision left abortion virtually inviolate until after the first trimester. *Webster* is filled with preoccupations about "fetal viability"—first articulated somewhat benignly in *Roe*. In *Webster* much of the legal discussion is centered on viability and the attendant tests required to determine same. Justice Sandra Day O'Connor found the trimester approach troubling in previous cases and introduced the notion of "undue burden." By that term she meant that as long as the tests, procedures, and the like did not place an undue burden on a woman's ability to have an abortion, such procedures or tests to assure fetus viability were not in conflict with *Roe*. The *Webster* decision more critically attacks the trimester approach and would in fact completely discard it, except, perhaps insofar as it offers a handy little "calendar" of when to begin the search for fetal viability.

The moment when a woman first feels movement or "life" in her womb is the basis for the search for fetal viability. Although this varies from pregnancy to pregnancy, it is most certainly not before twenty weeks. Given the state of Missouri's preamble, however, it seems irrelevant to argue about fetal viability, when presumably the state of Missouri would forbid all abortion as damaging to its fetal citizens, if *Roe* were not in its way. Chief Justice Rehnquist writes about the viability issue in the following way:

The viability-testing provision of the Missouri Act is concerned with promoting the State's interest in potential human life rather than in maternal health. Section 188.029 [of the Missouri Statute] creates what is essentially a presumption of viability at 20 weeks, which the physician must rebut with tests indicating that the fetus is not viable prior to performing an abortion. It also directs the physician's determination as to viability by specifying consideration, if feasible, of gestational age, fetal weight and lung capacity.

Such medical specificity, to say nothing of the theological arguments contained in the question of when life begins, do not belong in the proceedings of the Supreme Court. However much one disagrees morally or spiritually with abortion, a rational approach should be centered on the woman's right to control the destiny of her own life and her own body. As we have noted elsewhere, however, not only are women of childbearing age people with a set of expectations about their privacy, they are the only members of our society on which its very continuation is dependent. It is the equation of women with motherhood which makes privacy in pregnancy so untenable and, it would appear, temporary.

Interestingly, the plurality of the justices also believe that abortion has little place in the Court; however, they name the "rigid Roe framework" as the culprit. They especially cite the complexity of the trimester approach, which was an approach utilized in *Roe* for the specific purpose of balancing, in as fair a way as possible, the rights of women against the sanctity of life in the womb. In Chief Justice Rehnquist's words:

> The key elements of the Roe framework—trimesters and viability—are not found in the text of the Constitution or in any place else one would expect to find a constitutional principle. Since the bounds of the inquiry are essentially indeterminate, the result has been a web of legal rules that have become increasingly intricate, resembling a code of regulations rather than a body of constitutional doctrine.

The abandonment of the trimester approach, in all but the most superficial way, opens the door for intrusion into the lives of pregnant women. Ironically, they indicate that the notion of trimesters does not appear as a constitutional principle anywhere in our sacred document. However, these justices fail to see that what is embodied in the Constitution is precisely the issue they fail to acknowledge—that is, the clear separation of church and state. A Supreme Court opinion that begins with the theological tenet that life begins at conception and ends with a dissent citing no less than the authority of St. Thomas Aquinas must surely awaken the Deist and atheist fathers of the Constitution from their eternal slumber.

Privacy: For Sale to the Highest Bidder

In many ways the 1989 *Webster* ruling is as much an anti-civil rights decision as it is an anti-choice one, and it moves us back in time. Perhaps more than any of the other cases surrounding abortion, *Webster* more clearly and even more cruelly than the preceding decisions separates the privileged from the poor. Increasingly, the remaining constitutional entitlements to abortion are most readily accessible to those who are both crafty enough and wealthy enough to work around the restrictive ruling of the Court. *Webster* symbolizes a retreat from the movement toward equality for all citizens.

What does the *Webster* case say that makes it so hatefully balanced against all women—and particularly against poor, working, and lower middle class women who may desire an abortion? In some ways, *Webster* presents the classic distinction of the public/private dichotomy in American life and underlines the vast inequities of a system that has largely opted to advertise privacy and its attendant rights as commodities for sale. One of the crucial questions in *Webster* centers around the degree to which public facilities should be available for abortion.

Webster attacks women's rights in two fundamental ways. First, the decision by implication and application places more value on unborn life than on existing life. It is the woman as potential mother who is more likely to gain the state's sympathy than the woman qua woman. Second, *Webster* exacerbates the already dim condition of rights for those without resources by its restrictive holding with regard to public health facilities.

The most devastating aspect of *Webster* is its upholding of Missouri's restriction on the use of public facilities to perform abortions. Still clinging to its belief that to deprive a woman of the aid required to have an abortion does not deprive a woman of the right to an abortion, the Court has laid the groundwork for the complete reversal of *Roe*. First the funds, now the facilities; or in the Chief Justice's own words:

> Having held that the State's refusal to fund abortions does not violate *Roe v. Wade,* it strains logic to reach a

contrary result for the use of public facilities and em-
ployees. If the State may make a *value judgment* favoring
childbirth over abortion and ... implement that by the
allocation of public funds [in *Maher*], surely it [the State]
may do so through the allocation of other public resources, such as hospitals and medical staff. [my em-
phasis]

The prohibition against the use of public facilities for
abortion procedures can restrict the activities of private
hospitals as well. For example, as the Court has cited,
when a private hospital is constructed on leased public
lands (not an uncommon occurrence) abortions might be
restricted in such facilities. Apparently, the right to liberty and the exercise of one's civil rights is undiminished as
long as it is confined to private quarters and does not
occur within the public's view.

Whether or not the Court intended it, the "value judgment" they upheld in *Webster* by application will deprive
a substantial number of women from the full exercise of
their rights. Whatever the precise legal language of
Webster, what it says in practical terms to poor women, as
well as to millions of other women who live at somewhat
less marginal economic levels, is that they are not entitled
to as many choices and options for their lives as others
because they cannot pay the price attached to the exercise
of liberty. It is well to remember that factors other than
economic ones foreclose abortion as an option. Almost 80
percent of the abortions in this country are performed in
urban centers or metropolitan areas. The rural woman,

far from the urban center, may have an especially difficult time obtaining an abortion as increasingly few rural doctors perform them.

Lunch Counters or Hospitals: Deprivation of Access Is the Deprivation of Civil Rights

The Court, in its *Webster* decision, refers often to a woman's "choice," but not the kind of choice we have come to understand as a crucial ingredient to a woman's rights under the law.

> Missouri's refusal to allow public employees to perform abortions in public hospitals leaves a pregnant woman with the same choice *as if the State had chosen not to operate any public hospitals at all.* The challenged provisions only restrict a woman's ability to obtain an abortion to the extent *that she chooses to use a physician affiliated with a public hospital.* [my emphasis]

The Court's repeated use of the notion of choice in its restrictive abortion decisions (in funding and now in facilities) betrays the meaning of the word. A poor woman, from an urban area or from a rural one, would hardly describe herself as choosing a "physician affiliated with a public hospital." Her choice, under the meaning of *Webster*, will be to try desperately to find someone who will help her, knowing she might be unsuccessful or fall into dangerous hands, or to tough out an unwanted pregnancy.

What of this "state" without services, which is the creation and conception of the Court? This "state" cannot and does not exist, for the "state" has previously chosen to operate public hospitals and continues to do so. Thus to deprive a woman of the use of that public facility to exercise a constitutional right guaranteed under *Roe* is to deprive her of a civil right as a citizen. Deference to the institution of the Supreme Court notwithstanding, the logic of the plurality in this decision is an exercise in employing roadside carnival distortion mirrors. The simple and inescapable fact remains that as a nation we have provided public hospitals for the use of those who need them; the denial of access to them is a violation of one's civil rights. The fact that the denial is to women alone in this instance constitutes a violent discriminatory practice. What is the purpose of the "state" if not to provide a variety of institutions for the well-being of its citizens? What is the significance of the exercise of one's liberties and rights if the public settings have a "closed" sign posted on them?

Whatever forces conspire together to foreclose the option of choice for a woman (be they legal, economic, geographic, or the like) also deprive her of her rightful claim to equal protection, to due process, to an egalitarian life. What is the meaning of the exercise of liberty? Historically, American battles for rights have been fought around the use of facilities and services provided by the state. Where is this mythical nation the justices refer to when they speak of a place where women have just as many options as if the state did not provide funds, facilities, and the like? A state without such services is a creation of jurisprudence, not grounded in everyday reality.

At present, there is much debate and considerable hope about the French abortion pill RU486, known sometimes as the "morning after pill." While its availability in America would be a good thing for women, it is not the solution to our problems, nor a panacea to the abortion struggle. Technology does not resolve inequality nor does it reduce the intensity of ideological and religious political battles.

There is no reason to believe that RU486 will be readily available to all women, since the same problems of access and resources will come into play. The pill must be administered by a doctor, with the appropriate follow-up medical examinations. The women who have been denied federal funds for abortion, and now are denied access to public institutions, undoubtedly will be the same women denied the ability to obtain the medical treatment associated with this method of pregnancy termination.

Whether abortion comes dressed in the surgeon's smock or encased in a small vial of pills, the anti-choice advocates will continue to see any termination of pregnancy as the murder of life. Sadly, RU486, although it may be a medical miracle, will not cure our problems.

Black children were entitled to go to decent schools; the state had provided such schools but black students were excluded. Black children needed to have access to those facilities in order to be enfranchised citizens in the largest sense of that word. The war we have come to call the civil rights movement was based on that sense of equality and entitlement. Lunch counters and restaurants, while not state-owned but nonetheless public, also became a battleground for the civil rights struggle. The battle for liberty and equality has always been fought around access to public services, facilities, and resources. What can be the meaning of the right to choose an abortion if it must finally end up that it can only happen in one's own home or in expensive private and exclusive hospitals? If taken to its logical extension, that is the unmistakable presumption and direction of *Webster*.

Privacy in Pregnancy:
A Weapon or a Shield?

The *Webster* decision attacked the foundation of *Roe*, but it did not overturn it. It was only Justice Scalia who minced no words in saying that he would vote to rescind *Roe*, if given the opportunity to do so, and indeed held that not to do so within the *Webster* case was a mistake.

> The outcome of today's case will doubtless be heralded as a triumph of judicial statesmanship. It is not that, unless it is statesmanlike needlessly to prolong this Court's self-awarded sovereignty over a field where it has little proper business since the answers to most of the cruel questions posed are political and not juridical. . . .

It is Justice Scalia's opinion that may, more than the others, point the way to the shape of the future decisions of the Court. Opposed as he is to the law under the *Roe* precedent, Scalia in some senses acknowledges the sturdy construction of the "house" that Justice Blackmun built in that historic decision when he concludes his opinion with the following:

> It thus appears that the mansion of constitutionalized abortion-law, constructed overnight in *Roe v. Wade*, must be disassembled door-jamb by door-jamb, and never entirely brought down, no matter how wrong it may be.

As I have indicated in the preceding pages, the safe shelter constructed for women under *Roe* already had a few of its rooms removed in the cases that restricted funding. From the beginning of those restrictive rulings, it has been the poor and the economically marginal women most damaged. And this is precisely what the Court continued to do in the *Webster* case; this time it is a more aggressive and more complete attack, but it follows consistently and inevitably from the previous decisions limiting access to abortion, staying on the high and dry plane of theoretical judicial reasoning. The notion that to forbid the use of public funds for an abortion in no way detracts from the meaning and intent of *Roe* is a shadow game of rationality. Why does the Court's constitutional findings matter, with regard to abortion, if there is absolutely no way for a woman to finance one and if she is now also barred from using public facilities, which are the only ones available to her economically?

Abortion does not belong in the Constitution, presidential politics, or back alleys. Common sense and the realization that only those who desire an abortion need have one ought to be a rallying cry for people of varying ideologies and religious beliefs, who nonetheless agree that there are some things so private, so intimate, and, yes, so sacred that they belong inside the person's conscience and not in the public decision chambers or broadcast on the television news night after night. Quite clearly the Supreme Court, having taken the strategy it does in *Webster*, cannot be looked on to continue to condone abortion as part of a woman's constitutional rights under substantive privacy. *Webster* rejects the trimester analysis; it suggests that a full understanding of larger Constitutional principles of life, liberty, and so forth ought not to be a part of the consideration in abortion and virtually retreats from honoring a code of human decency through privacy as it applies to women.

Perhaps the New Right's well-oiled, but quite hysterical, anti-abortion forces will go too far. The hundreds of thousands who did take to the streets to march in Washington in April 1989, while confused that "getting your laws off my body" is where this whole mess started, nonetheless scream out by their numbers and their anger that women will not be silenced.

The forces of manipulation are now in full swing— that is, who can outwit what the Court really meant in this decision, and which side can most effectively use the Court's language to their benefit. There is no doubt that the right-to-life forces scored an enormous victory with *Webster* and one whose impact will be most severely felt by the poor and the working class. The "holy weapon" of the anti-abortion forces has been chiseled into a very sharp sword indeed by this decision of the Court. There is little question that until there is a redress of *Webster* these forces will most surely manipulate and control the lives of many women.

A Fetus Has the Right to Abortion

In 1962 an Arizona woman named Sheri Finkbine helped alert the population to the need for abortion reform. She was the first publicized victim of thalidomide use. Pregnant, and fearful that she would give birth to a badly deformed infant, she tried unsuccessfully to obtain an abortion in Arizona. Finkbine's plight was over-publicized, and although there were apparently sufficient provisions within the structure of Arizona law to enable her to have an abortion, she was unable to have one in her home state. Instead, with much press fanfare, she fled to Sweden, where she successfully aborted a seriously deformed fetus. People began then, in a most vivid way, to see the ramifications of restrictive abortion policy. What were we up to as a society? Should a woman, already a mother of four children, have to flee her own country like a fugitive to obtain an abortion?

There are fewer Sheri Finkbines these days—fewer compelling cases hit the media that point so sympathetically to a woman's need to abort and that mobilize human sentiment in quite the way the Finkbine case did. Usually we hear about the bitterness of the abortion battle—prayer breakfasts over pails of fetuses and the resilience of the anti-choice crusaders. Perhaps the stories that most compel public sentiment are those about the decisions regarding the unborn and the born. Who can be born; who should be born; who or what is a mother; and the like. Although we may try to separate the struggle for choice from the questions and quandaries coming out of birth technology, they have become increasingly merged.

A particularly moving voice of the right to choose is Mary Steichen Calderone, the physician and activist. Attempting to remobilize a sentiment of sympathy for abortion, she has called for the right of a fetus not to be born.

As a physician, I can see reasons both for and against abortion. But there is one person whose right to abortion has not ever been recognized, much less considered or met; a fetus that has been damaged before birth and will never have a chance for a normal life. My concern is for the rights of such innocent fetuses *not* to be born.

As a Quaker, I recollect words in the New Testament that express a haunted concern for the comforting of suffering fellow humans who are frighteningly trapped by inevitable life tragedies. . . . Such words illuminate

41

how one hard life road might be eased by the loving
charity of fellow humans willing to grant to a distorted
fetus the human right not to be born.

New York Times, Sept. 16, 1989

Whose Pregnancy? The Male
Claim for Control

Husbands, current and past, believing that they should
have the right to exert control over the question of a
woman's reproduction are not a new phenomenon. Lately, men who want to prevent a woman from aborting
claim that for a woman to exercise control over her body,
and her life options, somehow deprives a man of his "reproductive rights." In 1988 the *New York Times* began to
note the trend. Dateline: Garden City, Long Island, April
21, 1988—FATHERS ARE SEEKING MORE CONTROL OVER PREG-
NANCY. This article reported that an orthodontist had
filed a suit against his wife, seeking both a divorce and
monetary damages because she had an abortion without
his knowledge or consent. "It is the third case in as many
weeks in which men across the nation have argued that
fathers-to-be should have a say over whether a pregnant
woman may have an abortion."

This story illustrates how vulnerable women really are
to legal attacks and to public exposure by those who
would decide for them, even if it is one's husband, or
former husband. While *Roe* revolutionized a part of
women's lives, it was not a radical system of privacy. For

privacy to work, post-*Roe* and most assuredly post-*Webster* it still demands that others honor the primacy of another's claim to control and to privacy. In order to truly control your own life, you must be able to maintain privacy over certain functions.

In marriage a partner can use privacy as a weapon in another way, as in "You had no right to do this privately." Thus one's personal behavior can be condemned as inappropriately private, even within the confines of an intimate realm. In the case of the orthodontist, the claim was that it should have been the husband's business as well. The attorney representing the wife argued that the husband was using the abortion as a ploy to lessen the amount of support payments he would have to pay. In any event, the man in this instance employed a dramatic invocation of his rights, accusing the wife of a "wrongfully private" act: "This is a case of father's rights, of husband's rights. . . . It is a case of an outrageous act that a wife did against a husband. Without my knowledge, without my consent, she took our baby and ripped it out of her."

The story, which appeared prominently on page two of the *New York Times*, was accompanied by a picture of the couple in happier days, the kind of photo one sees in scrapbooks or family photo albums, snapped at a grand party or on a cruise or on their honeymoon. Here it is for all of us to view with our morning coffee: Couple in trouble, it says to us, in trouble over the most intimate decision a woman probably ever makes. She is being sued by her own husband in a dispute over the legitimacy of the "secrecy" of her action—his claim that inside marriage there should be a rightful, even legal, demand for revelation of pregnancy, and the prevention of abortion by a husband.

The Great Collision: Privacy and Control

Privacy and control belong together; they work together for ultimate power. As a symbol, privacy is a sacred shield that a person can use to protect the self. Yet privacy also functions symbolically as a holy weapon to use against others. To invade another's life by intruding on his or her private affairs is to utilize this weapon to gain control over their lives. Why the phrase "holy weapon"? Because the invasion or intrusion is usually done in the name of a greater good or a greater cause. Privacy invasions are virtually always justified for a higher moral purpose or public good or for a nobler motivation than privacy protection. The many-pronged right-to-life movement claims the highest good of all, "life," over the greatest evil, "murder." These invasions of privacy are pursued for the supposed protection of something precious. Nowhere is the metaphor of holy weapon as appropriate as it is when applied to the forces of the right-to-life movement who, using the concept of the sacredness of "life," mask their actual intent, which is to successfully manipulate, control, and damage other people's lives.

The Rise of the Fetal Citizen

The attachment to fetal life is a peculiar obsession in America. Those citizens who are compelled to protect the unformed life inside a woman's womb are precisely those most likely to approve of the idea that ketchup should qualify as a food group for children receiving federal lunch programs. (During the Reagan presidency, there was, in fact, such a proposal with regard to those children qualifying for the federal hot lunch program.) For the members of the right-to-life movement, the fetal citizen has obtained more rights and consideration than will ever again be granted from that group. For these anti-abortion advocates, the state's compelling interest in human life stops at birth, it would seem, with little worry or funds devoted to assisting a child once it is born.

It is also worth remembering that not too many years ago a macabre little right-to-life sideshow went from town to town, with dozens of tiny caskets symbolizing dead fetuses, and at each stop conducted ritualized funeral services for these dead tissues. The pro-choice march on Washington in April 1989 mobilized the opposition to place hundreds of tiny markers in a mock graveyard for the fetal dead.

The privacy of pregnancy, long understood as a common right, is a phenomenon of times gone by. Even during periods of primitive or barbarian birthing practices, there prevailed the notion and the reality of the "mother's child" inside her womb. Why is the concept of the "mother's child" an important tool for women? Because it leaves a woman to her own conscience, to fate, and to the available medical knowledge and technology of the times. The death of the child-of-the-womb has given rise to the birth of the fetal citizen, and with the creation of this pre-born, presentient, and invisible citizenry, a legitimate expectation of privacy in pregnancy has been thrown out.

Part Two

The Opening of the American Womb

When the womb itself was such a very private place and pregnancy so mysterious, the logic of privacy in pregnancy was more obvious. It was easier to defend and to comprehend that here was a place where the legitimate expectation of privacy was specifically applicable. Although abortion was not made part of our national legal structure until *Roe*, the fact of privacy in pregnancy existed by a kind of community consent. While not acknowledged by the Court per se, the recognition of a privacy entitlement in family matters extended to most aspects of pregnancy. Medical technology, from reproductive magic such as in-vitro fertilization or surrogate mothering to the now more routine and mundane procedures of sonograms and amniocentesis, has opened up a Pandora's box. Hypothetical scenarios are now reality. All of this forces us to question whether it will ever again be possible to create privacy for women in their pregnancies, or in the womb itself.

Andrew Malcolm talks of the change in the following way:

> [Pregnancy] ended wondrously, with painful hopes, in the beginning of a new life, a baby whose sex wasn't known until the moment of birth. Now, of course, thanks to science and technology, much of that has changed. Sperm is donated and screened. Eggs are plucked or targeted at the ripest moment. Wombs are rented. Fertilization occurs in lab dishes. Embryos are frozen for future use. Fetuses, swimming about in utero, are routinely viewed on television screens, *their developing organs monitored while the room is filled with the stereophonic sound of an unborn heart whooshing toward maturity.* [my emphasis]
>
> *NY Times Book Review*, Jan. 1, 1989

The Fight for Fetal Status

In his book *Science and the Unborn*, the biologist Clifford Grobstein reminds us that the assignment of status is very important to a society's workings. One's status determines the degree of freedom, amount of protection, number of entitlements, and the general quality of life a person can reasonably expect. How many rights a society accords you, and the accompanying privileges and guarantees that derive from those rights, or your ability to redress unfairness or mistreatment, flow rather directly from your status. In America, animals (especially domestic pets and the smaller furry animals) have been accorded a special kind of status, as part of our somewhat generalized romantic notion of animal life. The status of domestic pets in particular has led to their special handling and to their protection through laws. The creation of the ASPCA, as well as advocacy groups monitoring medical and cosmetic industry experimentation with animals, and extending beyond to those groups who aggressively oppose the fur industry, come largely from the status we have assigned to animals in our culture.

A great deal rises or falls on what status your existence is assigned by common understanding, by consensus, or by law. Much of what we are, the determination of our very existence, is part of an ascribed status. Ascribed status consists of involuntary qualities and attributes that cannot be changed essentially. A white or black person is a member of that race for life. While the ranking of one's race may change by law or political mood, and thereby the accompanying rights, benefits, exclusions, or punishments, the fact of one's race is a permanent tag or social identifier. On the other hand, a few of the things that comprise our being belong to a voluntary category of identity and are largely behavioral manifestations that can be changed. A young male who identifies as a punk-rocker and dresses accordingly might feel a certain temporary diminution in the way he is treated when he walks into an elegant, expensive restaurant. This status, however, is a voluntary one, which the individual may choose to change with mood or peer group and thereby alter dramatically the way he would be treated if he were to enter the same restaurant again.

What we as a society finally, collectively come to call unborn human cells will determine their status and therefore the kinds of policies and ethics that will be employed in their handling. Status is the vehicle that drives policy and ethics. That is the *genius*, if you will, of the right-to-life movement. They insist that these cells be given a permanent ascribed status of unborn human life or, as they are fond of saying, "preborn children." From their vantage point, the status of a human life is a constant, whether these cells are in a womb, petri dish, or frozen forever in a solution of chemical preservatives.

Scientists argue strongly for a clarity of status for the unborn because the work of genetic scientists and the advances of medical reproductive technology will not stop in order for our laws and ethics to catch up, although they may be hindered somewhat by our profound confusions.

The importance of status as a far-reaching societal mechanism is not a new notion to the discipline of political theory. Status, as conferred by law, regulation, or convention, does determine rights and protections and sets up a common understanding or contract of agreement from which policy and a system of ethics might stem. There is hardly a question that the *scientific status* of unborn life changes vastly from the early stages of the fertilized egg or zygote through to the nine-month fetus. This form of life is unlike a fully formed person of a particular race or a specific gender; the fetus, and before that the embryo, is not static in its emerging and tentative status of "human life" but is constantly changing and developing. At issue here instead is our *cultural assignment* of status for unborn life, not its scientific definition alone.

We have come to a place where some would confer full

51

human status, and therefore its attendant rights, on the fetus, or even on the prefetus, or zygote. A zygote is, in lay terms, the result of a successful sperm-fertilized egg—in other words, the technical label for "conception."

With the advent of frozen reproductive technology, these little masses of cells, alive in the technical sense and human (in the scientific sense of their possessing humanly identifiable tissue, not chimpanzee or giraffe tissue), are championed by the right-to-life groups as humans needing protection. What a ghoulish notion to consider thousands of "parentless, homeless" frozen little zygotes far outliving the donors who created them or the doctors who preserved them, and thus providing a cause célèbre for zealots advocating a kind of prelife sanctification. If we are to take this seriously, their activities seem to mean that frozen zygotes have a right to exist indefinitely and to be protected by a full array of civil rights and liberties.

A zygote, frozen in time and place, is not, after all, an about-to-be-born, fully-gestated, nine-month fetus. Birth confers status, as Grobstein and others are quick to point out; but we are still left demanding to know where medical technology and wizardry has really left us. Scientists argue that the insistence that life begins at conception not only hampers a woman's right to choose an abortion but places undue burdens on fertility research itself.

What we do know pretty clearly, however, is that we have arrived at a ridiculous impasse where some would confer full human status and its attendant constitutional rights on the fetus, and even on the prefetus.

Difficult as it may be to comprehend rationally, at this point, there is a serious dialogue about whether or not the International Declaration on Human Rights protects laboratory-frozen zygotes. Can we engage in a serious debate that compares an aborted fetus, or destroyed zygote, to the wreckage of a woman's life who is forced to have a child she does not want or is incapable of raising? The Equal Rights Amendment for Women (ERA) failed; but now we are engaged in a national conversation (at the highest levels) about how fetuses might be protected by specific inclusion in the Constitution, while their adult pregnant women counterparts are not.

Reproductive Technology:
Friend or Foe?

Originally perceived as a good thing for women, reproductive technology has elevated the notion of motherhood. This elevation diminishes the public's approval of the abortion choice and may contribute to the lack of available and affordable abortions for many women. At the very least, technology has added to the complexity of the fight for abortion rights and underlined its now inescapably bitter and ideological aspects. Women who cannot have babies often want to have babies; this is not a new fact or recent developmental phase of human nature. In the past, women who craved the joys, rewards, and satisfactions commonly grouped together as perhaps uniquely found in motherhood had few options, other than adoption. Their "barren wombs" became a source of private sorrow or grief. The sages of the Bible dealt with our foremothers who found themselves in such a predicament with a delicate rhetorical hand.

Enter the last part of the twentieth century, and along comes reproductive technology; and we find that birth research can keep pace with other medical advancements, in some cases moving ahead of them. Abracadabra, we have rubbed a magical lantern that has produced a genie who gives women those wanted babies and who will tell them their sorrow may well be over. Childlessness need no longer be a permanent status. At the same time, another genie is out of the magic lamp forever, and this one assures us that privacy in pregnancy is a very outdated and dead custom. That dark mystery of life's beginning is now quite in the open and can never be returned to the land of shadows and whispers. Protecting a pregnant woman's privacy is a much tougher job with both the womb and the birth process in the public eye.

The miracle of birth may still be a miracle, but that part of the miracle attributed to the shroud of mystery is gone. Miraculous births are instead now documented because of technically assisted pregnancies. The notion of that dark, guarded, mysterious thing called pregnancy is no longer a part of our vernacular. A friend says these new events have ushered in the age of "kangaroo pregnancies"—we carry our young in our observable, almost external "birth pockets."

It is somewhat parallel to remember that in ancient

times, before man had figured out his direct involvement in the process of birth through the contribution of his sperm, women were thought to be sacred deities. This was the age of woman-as-goddess, because life appeared to spring forth from her, without assistance from anyone else. Once man recognized, or learned, of his critical involvement in the continuation of the species, women's star fell hard, fast, and a long way down. Today the public nature of reproduction through technologically assisted pregnancy has had much the same effect on a woman's entitlements.

All women are to some extent at the mercy of the technologies that on the surface purport to be for their benefit. As women first began to think seriously about pregnancy and motherhood without convention of marriage, or even a serious relationship with a man, some women attempted to inseminate themselves with sperm "donated" from male friends. The sociologist Norma J. Wikler has written about this phenomenon and labeled that time the age of "turkey-baster babies." Whether or not the homely old turkey baster was the technology employed by those women, the point is well taken. Those were private attempts—undoubtedly less successful, but also far less ridden with the complications of the above. Yet even those early and primitive attempts belong to this reproductive minefield.

In a newspaper column appearing not long after the *Webster* decision, William F. Buckley deftly captured an intellectual conservative's opposition to abortion, inextricably linking it to the medical advancements since the reasoning of the *Roe* decision.

> It is established now, much more clearly than 16 years ago, that the fetus by any measurement is a developing human being and as such a plausible contender for the right to protection, even as an infant who is a developing child, and a child, who is a developing adult, are all entitled to protections of various kinds . . . .
>
> If a fetus were nurtured in a test tube, it would be difficult to marshal arguments giving anyone the right to interrupt the flow of nutriment to that fetus. Given that in such a condition it assumes a particularity as a developing human being entitled to protection, the contention that although the vehicle of the development of the human being is the mother's womb, not the test tube, and therefore the fetus is no more the concern of protective legislation than a tomato, is difficult persuasively to contend.

Knowledge, long recognized as a source of power, has indeed empowered those who fight for the fetus. It is this same vast amount of knowledge, information, and the arsenal of sophisticated birth techniques that has lessened a woman's control of her own body and destiny, except within the confines of pregnancy, where her chances and options unquestionably have been increased. For women the new options, alternatives, and possibilities for achieving motherhood have been garnered at a considerable loss of her powers as a woman qua woman or as an independent and autonomous citizen. To return to the fairy tale analogy of the lantern and the genie, in such tales the fairy godmother or genie often warns the wisher just prior to granting the desire to "be sure of what you wish for, as you will get it." Reproductive technologies have so advanced the process of pregnancy that it is as though the womb has become dismembered from the woman in question as Buckley's "test-tube womb" analogy eerily suggests. The devices that have helped women get pregnant, and the techniques that have aided them in producing healthy babies, have in a profound and basic way made women far more vulnerable as human beings, apart from their biological function as reproductive units for society.

Pregnancy and desperation—these words go together hand in glove, but women are not mere "screaming wombs," indentured to that part of themselves. Society has been organized in a way that makes the desperation at once both understandable and inevitable. As our previous history suggests, and as women's self-help health clinics attest, women will search for a way not to go forward with an unwanted pregnancy. Lately, the other side of desperation has led women to engage in techniques more akin to animal husbandry than human reproduction in their attempts to become pregnant. To fill the womb, or to empty it—the desire to have or to get rid of pregnancy is an emotion and a motivation known and comprehended only by women of the species. It is an inescapable fact that a woman who had an abortion at twenty-two may be the same woman who at thirty-nine will utilize every method available to get pregnant and stay successfully so through to the birth of a healthy child.

Pregnancy, with all of its ramifications, is a solely female enterprise and an event that can be resolved only by individual female control and autonomy. At present, it dominates and predominates too much of our private and public life. Simone de Beauvoir long ago noted that freedom for women would be impossible until women could control their reproductive destinies. This is not a new thought; it predates de Beauvoir. Women for centuries have been engaged in this dialectic with their bodies. They have also understood the power of their reproductive capabilities. The play *Lysistrata* illustrates that at least one male has also understood.

Women now are less empowered by their reproductive capacity and more beleaguered by choices and the fight to maintain choices. The dialectic has moved far beyond the bodies of women. American history is a chronicle of women gaining and losing control over their reproduction. Despite our sophisticated technologies, women are essentially engaged in the same conversation with the state about their own reproduction that they were one hundred years ago.

As a society we have made an enormous commitment to the development of technologies that enable babies to be born against all odds. It is therefore a fairly straightforward causal line to argue that the state might not then feel, at some future date, that it can also have a compelling interest in "killing off" the little creatures they presently seem to be spending so much time, technological energy, and resources developing. The existence of these technologies, many of them developed with federal funds, says that the state's compelling interest in life predates birth. When such a big fuss is made about the very notion of getting women pregnant and keeping them successfully so, reproductive technology takes on a heroic character. In so doing a kind of personhood is invested in the fetus, whether or not that was the intent. The availability of reproductive technology has fueled and legitimated the claims of the anti-choice forces that a fetus is something more than mere tissue matter. The advancement of this peculiar kind of medical technology has complicated our morality and has confused what might be done *for* a fetus with what can or should be done *to* a fetus.

Reproductive technology has dramatically reformulated pregnancy and the concept of "mother." There is now the possibility that a genetic mother can be different from the gestational mother. There are numerous kinds of surrogate arrangements, implantation in other than the egg-donor mother, and a variety of other techniques available, all forcing the question, What is pregnancy about after all? Is pregnancy a stage of a woman's life or is it only the beginning stage of "another's" life? If we do, in the final analysis, opt for the latter, then where the unborn resides prior to its arrival is somewhat irrelevant.

Following that logic, the test tube, a natural genetic and gestational mother, or a woman under contract to produce a baby becomes secondary to the unborn. Obviously, the answer must be that pregnancy can be both things—a phase of a woman's life and the beginning of another life. Which aspect receives predominant validation or importance will, to a very large extent, define the terms of the discourse about reproductive liberty.

Pregnant for Whom?
From "Baby M" to a Global Maternal Sweatshop

During 1987 and part of 1988, the front pages of national newspapers and all television network news broadcasts covered the story of "Baby M," an infant carried to term and born to a woman named Mary Beth Whitehead, the surrogate mother—and genetic—mother. (In the case of Mary Beth Whitehead, the baby was the result of an artificial insemination of Bill Stern's sperm. Thus, Mary Beth Whitehead was the natural, or genetic, mother of Baby M.)

It took three courts to determine who was indeed the "mother." This was a child reproductive technology produced, and during the legal process of trying to determine to whom she belonged, the inside details of every character's life were revealed. Just how sick was Elizabeth Stern, the woman who sought to become a mother by contracting Mary Beth Whitehead to carry a fetus from her husband's sperm? Could she have, or should she have, risked a pregnancy? All aspects of the life of the biological mother, Mary Beth Whitehead, were revealed, even her relationship with her sister. No aspect of her life seemed too trivial to merit legal testimony and press coverage. What was at issue here? Motherhood or contract law? The concepts of motherhood and privacy were deeply confused and conflicted in a most vicious legal struggle, and advocates of women's rights often found themselves bitterly divided.

There has been concern for some time about the possibility, or perhaps the likelihood, that "human breeding farms" could be developed where the poor of the world would produce babies for the rich. A variety of scholars, philosophers, ethicists, and social scientists have suggested that women need protection from the abuses of reproductive technology. The incidence of poorly paid rural women in developing Third World countries working for multinational companies at a tiny fraction of what they would earn if they were employed in the urban headquarters of the corporation in question led the anthropologist Maria Patricia Fernandez-Kelly and the economist Saskia Sassen-Koop to coin the phrase "the global sweatshop." Without international regulations or codes on pregnancy, the feminist concern is that wombs might be for rent with little compensation and with the opportunity for great exploitation of the women attached to the wombs—a kind of maternal sweatshop.

Again we see the complexity of the trade-offs involved.

A code of regulations for the occurrence of pregnancy opens, of course, the possibility for the abuse of other freedoms and liberties. Yet to pretend that reproductive technology does not also open the avenue for a swift international trading business in the commodity of pregnancy and childbirth is a far too innocent view of reality or of the historical course of human nature.

My Zygote/Myself:
The Case of the Frozen Embryos

A Tennessean named Mary Sue Davis was desperate to become pregnant. She engaged in that effort for a little more than a decade. Beginning in 1979, after her marriage, she suffered a series of life-threatening pregnancies—including a ruptured fallopian tube due to a tubal pregnancy. Yet she and her husband persevered in their efforts to reproduce. With her husband's presumed concern and enthusiasm, they sought help from the reproductive magicians who successfully fertilized nine of Mrs. Davis's eggs, using her husband's sperm. Twice the implantation efforts failed. Seven remained; seven chances for a new Davis.

What did not remain was the stability of the Davis marriage. Junior Lee and Mary Sue divorced, and at issue were the remaining fertilized eggs—frozen embryos. Despite Mrs. Davis's promise that she wanted children, not financial support, Mr. Davis wanted nothing of it. Claiming he should also have the right to control his reproduction, in an overcharged and highly ironic statement Mr. Davis claimed he was "raped of my reproductive rights." Apparently left with no other options for a private resolution of the dispute, this Tennessee couple found themselves in that popular arena for intimate disputes, the courts.

The attorneys for Mrs. Davis argued that she was entitled to those last seven embryos, each about four to eight cells, looking not unlike mouse embryos. Indeed, she ought to be so entitled, many women's rights advocates would agree. Her own counsel, however, chose to argue, with the aid of expert witnesses, that these were the preborn children of Mrs. Davis. The judge, W. Dale Young, decided in favor of Mrs. Davis, and he did so on the grounds that these were "human beings existing as embryos." This was a victory for a woman named Mary Sue Davis; this was not a victory for women in the larger battle of reproductive freedom. The foundation of Mrs. Davis's claim, as advanced by her counsel and as extended and elaborated by the judge, did little to advance the notion of choice, or of privacy in pregnancy.

In language echoing much of the tone of *Webster*, Judge W. Dale Young stated that life begins at conception, even frozen conception, and even conception occurring outside the womb. The overriding interest of the state is the best interest of the "child," according to Judge Young. Judicially wise Justice Young denounced any link to *Webster*, pointedly saying that the Supreme Court had dealt only with abortion and not with medical technologies. His protest is particularly unconvincing in this regard; the connection between *Webster* and a case like *Davis v. Davis* is unmistakable. The state, writ large, believes that life begins at conception; the specific state of Tennessee now believes that applies to life, even four cells out of the womb, and concludes that its only concern must be for the best interests of the "child."

Try as I might, I am unable to see the child or even to visualize it. Where is the child the judge refers to—seven frozen embryos, any one of which might be selected in the next pregnancy attempt of Mrs. Davis? To talk of these unformed cells, frozen and undifferentiated, as though they constitute an engaging, vulnerable little child caught up in a custody battle is just so much nonsense. It is all too reminiscent of the Edward Albee play *Who's Afraid of Virginia Woolf?* A great deal of the drama of that play revolved around an imaginary child of the central characters, George and Martha. This "child" provides much of the vitriolic focus in the dance of death between George and Martha. As they each attempt to destroy the other emotionally, they employ this "child" as a weapon. In the end, in a hatefully powerful scene, George "kills off" the child. The play is a brilliant tour de force by a master playwright who so clearly articulated the absurdity of life.

Theater of the absurd? Perhaps. However, the definition of frozen embryos as children in need of the state's loving care is not much less absurd than the antics of George and Martha. What is so troubling is the judge's ease in defining such tissue masses as children and, astoundingly, saying, "The full focus of the court in the case of children is on what's to their best interests, not what Mom wants, not what Dad wants, and not what the grandparents want."

What else might Judge Young have done? He might have decided against Mrs. Davis and for Mr. Davis, and then fought over what should be done with the frozen embryos. He might have decided that this was a property dispute and not a child custody case, despite Mrs. Davis's lawyers' argument. In that instance, he might have concluded, as is often the case in marital property disputes, that the person who would be most damaged by the deprivation of this property was Mrs. Davis. We have a problem with this argument in America. It makes us queasy. Anything mildly resembling human life being labeled as property causes us to recall the days when women, blacks, and children were all categorized as property. Perhaps for those who adhere strictly to the notion that birth, and only birth, can confer human status, the property definition is less troublesome, especially when applied to groups of cells as yet so unformed that they have not even begun to separate into differentiated cells.

Yet the judge did have another option, which, if taken, would have gone a long way to restoring women's autonomy and weakening the link between the right-to-life forces and medical technology, and would have eliminated the problem of defining zygotes as property. He might simply have said, "This is a woman's decision—if she wants to try seven more times to get pregnant and is willing to take those physical and emotional risks—that choice is hers." No discussion of property, or of the status of unborn life. Simply a woman's choice to attempt to get pregnant and stay pregnant. If we are busily working up ethical surrogacy contracts for pregnancies, surely a contract might have been drawn up for Mr. Davis which would have held him harmless from any claims from Mrs. Davis and wherein he could have relinquished his paternity rights. A contract that granted Mary Sue Davis the right to those embryos might have been created in a manner that would not have exaggerated the whole conflict into another theological argument about when life begins, which now seems to find its place not in the catechisms of faith but in the courtrooms of this country.

Who is the enemy to women in the Davis case? It is a complicated answer. In some basic way, as noted, Mrs. Davis herself, in her victory, undermined much of the foundation for the claim for a woman's jurisdiction over her pregnancy because she resorted to the hysterical and emotionally loaded tactic of claiming these embryos as "her children." The analogue provided in this case from anti-abortion to technology points to a loss of choice for women, as interpreted by the courts. Interestingly, the lawyers for Mr. Davis argued that the embryos were property, a far less palatable approach than had the self-same argument been made by the woman in this case.

Discussing embryo development, Charles Gardner, a researcher at the University of Michigan Medical School, makes even more ludicrous the discussion of embryo-as-child:

> The early human embryo, like the mouse, is a ball of cells .... The nature of embryonic development makes it impossible to think of an egg or a cluster of cells as a person. Time itself must be woven into the fabric of the embryo before it becomes a baby.... The embryo is not a child. It is not a baby. It is not yet a human being.
>
> *The Nation,* Nov. 13, 1989

Womb Versus Woman

How do we find a way to select those destined to be born? How does a society choose who should make those decisions, without resulting in the kind of warfare we currently see on the front lines of the abortion battle?

It is hard to argue that on the one hand the unborn are nothing more than bunches of shapeless, meaningless tissue blobs, and on the other hand that incredibly expensive, potentially dangerous, and very sophisticated medical treatments should be developed in order to test and sustain the life of those fetuses destined for babyhood. We spend vast amounts of dollars and medical energy to keep desperately premature babies alive even when the likelihood of their enjoyment of a full life is extremely small. The advent of "fetal surgery," in which corrective measures can be performed on the developing fetus in utero, is another example of pregnancy's modern paradox.*

We face the dilemma of defining or separating the unborn from the unformed. Technology and *Roe* have all helped to pit the fetus against the mother. The rise of this fetal citizenry has surely been aided by the somewhat miraculous, but also often grisly, things that can go on with regard to preformed, unborn living tissues, both inside and outside the womb.

The possibility of "selective abortion" highlights this point. When a woman is pregnant with multiple fetuses (almost always the result of fertility drugs or embryo implantation), one or more of the fetuses may be seen as weak, with little chance of survival. It is also often the case that to continue to carry all the fetuses would result in a total miscarriage of the pregnancy. Thus doctors are confronted with the task of "reducing" quadruplets to twins, for example. Additionally, of course, many women would not choose to have *five* babies, however desperately they wanted *one*.

---

*Diagnosis of fetal defects can now be ascertained in the early weeks of pregnancy—increasingly at the fifth and sixth weeks. An English experiment conducted at the Medical Research Council Laboratory in London diagnosed defects in *three-day-old* mouse embryos. The medical journal *Lancet* reported the experiment, pointing to its relevance for human reproduction. If successful, this technique could be used in human fertilization methods, and the "test-tube" embryos could be tested for genetic defects *before* implantation in the womb.

If a selective abortion of two or three fetuses allows a woman the chance to be the mother of healthy twins, the ethical dilemma is reduced. If, however, the abortion of multiple fetuses is only because that number of children is unacceptable, some physicians are more tentative than in the case of a single-fetus abortion, when the woman wants no children. According to Gina Kolata (*New York Times*, January 1988):

> Many doctors and ethicists who disapprove of most abortions of healthy fetuses say they can justify the new procedure in some circumstances. Yet something about it saddens even those who accept ordinary abortions. . . . What is troubling is the prospect of a woman trying for years to become pregnant, undergoing enormous emotional strain and financial sacrifice to have a family of her own, and then ending up having to kill perfectly healthy fetuses.

Dr. Joseph Schulman, director of the Genetics and IVF Institute in Fairfax, Virginia, who said he has no problem with abortions in general, once observed another doctor reduce quadruplets to twins. "It was not a pleasant sight," he said. Technology gives us more choices, but we may be ill equipped to deal with its unpleasant or painful ramifications. Reproductive technology has gone far beyond the individual woman's choice.

Technology now provides the opportunity to test and to monitor all that is wrong and all that may go wrong in a pregnancy. Perhaps the day will dawn when the decision of a diabetic woman whether or not to have a child will be the state's choice, not hers. It raises the possibility of the creation and maintenance of a "genetic underclass," as social analyst Dorothy Nelkin has termed it. The monitoring of the lives of pregnant women through technology allows us to ask the question "If you cannot produce a perfect child, why bother?" The question of who will answer the "why bother" is of particular concern to the continuation of privacy.

The focus on the unborn has pushed liberals and feminists into an impossible ideological paradox. If, through the protection of the liberties of the existing people on the planet, those protecting privacy in pregnancy are made to look like callous, unfeeling bullies, something has gone quite awry in our configuration. Advocates of individual liberty in the area of pregnancy may hear the echo of the nasty old Social Darwinist quip "The drunk is in the gutter where he belongs—leave him there." If we are boxed into an either/or dichotomy of *woman versus fetus*, those protecting the privacy rights of the living sound a bit like that with regard to unborn life. A way must be found to conquer this dichotomous way of thinking (mother versus fetus) so that we might come forward into this age of technology, and terror, with a new model for pregnancy.

Families used to guard their own histories, choosing which events they might reveal at an appropriate time and to whom. Families have less control over their secrets now because they have diminishing power to influence the direction of their intimate decisions. The idea that a husband or a family might have to choose between the life of the wife and mother and an about-to-be-born child is a grief-ridden decision. That sorrow has become now a matter of public debate, and even litigation. Strangers appoint themselves "guardians" of a fetus and file legal actions to prevent abortion, or to force doctors to perform cesarean sections.

Martin Klein, a Long Island, New York, man, was forced into court in a series of battles against the right-to-life forces that ended ultimately with intervention from the Supreme Court. In two weeks of publicity and hell, this man fought for his wife's life against strangers whose sole concern was the life of the unborn fetus. His pregnant wife, Nancy, had been critically injured in an automobile accident and was comatose; the doctors said the pregnancy increased the strain on her delicate system. If an abortion were performed there was some hope for recovery. Yet the ferocious pro-fetal forces, in a perversion of the notion of family, quickly assumed the now familiar pseudofamilial role of "guardians" of the fetus and tried to block the abortion. Eventually, the husband prevailed, and the Court granted the husband the right to order an abortion for his wife and appointed him Nancy Klein's legal guardian. While Mr. Klein did prevail, it was not before he had been dragged through a relentlessly expensive and inherently exhausting public legal process— and not before his grief, the details of his wife's accident and medical condition, and divergent views of the prognosis of her pregnancy and its harm to his wife had been front-page news and dinner-hour television viewing. (Nancy Klein, by the way, did emerge from the coma following the abortion, and although progress is slow, she is recovering her movement, her memory, and her ability to speak. There is no argument but that the abortion aided her developmental recovery.)

The appellate division court of the state of New York granted Klein guardianship over his then comatose wife and said, "These [the anti-abortion advocates] are absolute strangers to the Klein family.... " Yet these strangers, undeterred, attempted to block the abortion by appealing the lower court's decision to the Supreme Court. It was Justice Thurgood Marshall who finally stopped them when he denied their appeal to forbid the abortion. In a further example of just how far from the mainstream these activists are, New York City's Cardinal John J. O'Connor, the powerful and vocal opponent of abortion, said that he could not condemn the decision of the husband in this instance. "If I were the lady's husband and the father of that child, I would be terribly torn ... the Church indicts no one." While he obviously was not condoning abortion, nor overtly approving of it even in this extreme case, what is noteworthy is how far from the opposition Cardinal O'Connor placed himself. He avoided any reference to their activity, to the lawsuit filed against the Klein family, or to the larger abortion issue, limiting his remarks instead to sympathetic ones aimed at the family and their personal tragedy.

This case, while individually painfully dramatic, must be placed within the context of the anti-abortion battle. The Klein family simply presented these right-to-life militants with a convenient vehicle for their efforts. If this particular woman was caught in the middle, and potentially harmed by their activities, so be it. This case, perhaps even more than others, illustrates the naked disregard the most radical elements of the right-to-life element have with respect to the actual life of the living woman.

The people who fought against the Klein family were Lawrence Washburn and John Short, professional anti-abortionists. Short came to public attention some time ago in the early 1970s when, as an accountant for the Nassau, Long Island, Department of Social Services, he engaged in a form of civil disobedience by refusing to process the medical claims for abortions done at the Nassau County Medical Center. He was fired, but he later hired the attorney Washburn to represent him against the county. Short's victory was sweet, in his eyes. He was made legal guardian for any fetuses born alive in late-term abortions at the Nassau County Medical Center.

Mr. Washburn has an even longer vita in the role of fake family friend. Washburn came to national attention in 1983 when he managed to drag a tragedy-ridden family into court with regard to medical treatment of a hopelessly impaired infant. The press called the baby "Baby Jane Doe," and in many ways Baby Doe not only began Mr. Washburn's career but ushered in the age of strangers posing as friends of the defenseless. Increasingly, that has come to mean "defending" the fetuses of pregnant women. Why is this even legally possible? Because too many states, New York being one of them, have ambiguous laws relating to incapacitated or disabled people, making it possible for anyone to apply to be their legal guardians. After his defeat in the Klein case, Mr. Washburn's comment was both telling and startling: "Each precedent that limits our power to protect unborns is a setback. . . . "

The legal journalist Marcia Chambers provided an illuminating insight into this case in "The Politics of Abortion in the Courts" (*The National Law Journal*, vol. II, no. 27, 13 March 1989): To understand the political, rather than the constitutional or privacy, dimensions of the Klein case is to know the judicial and municipal cast of characters. Chambers reports that the right-to-life forces in New York's Nassau County are well organized and politically efficacious. They elect judges, and other officials. The Nassau County district attorney at the time was one of their own. Denis Dillon, that district attorney, saw the Klein abortion as homicide, because of his anti-abortion ideology. Therefore, when the hearing on Klein's order to show cause why he should not be his wife's guardian came before a judge, it came before one Bernard McCaffrey, a judge who had won on a right-to-life ticket. That made a particularly hospitable environment for Washburn, Short, and their colleagues, who, were . . . "within a day . . . with no standing whatsoever, welcomed into the case by the judge." Chambers's concluding remarks are particularly insightful:

> There is a lot to be learned from this case about politics and legal procedure, about the value of delay and publicity. Behind the legal circumlocution, the judges in this case knew full well who should be represented in court, and who shouldn't be. So did Mr. Dillon. . . . But a hearing was played out, it seems, in order to give the interlopers a national stage and a national audience. They received the kind of publicity they could not buy and they got it at a time when the nation's abortion law is under siege.

Fetal Neglect:
The Ultimate Accusation

Technology has revealed the mystery of life. This revelation has been politically distorted by the strident prolifers who believe they have unveiled life's true genesis and meaning, notwithstanding the scientific evidence to the contrary. The open womb—what has it accomplished? One of its downsides is the ability to conjure up the image and the accusation of the "bad mother" all the earlier. The neglectful mother, the abusing mother— these are powerful and incriminating labels. Some children are mercilessly pummeled by disturbed parents, left to fend for themselves in abandoned houses, scalded in hot water, and other horrors. The tabloids, the respectable daily newspapers, the local television news, all vividly and graphically report that vast numbers of children are neglected and abused. And sadly, women, mothers, are sometimes the culprits. But the notion that a woman can be accused of and charged with child abuse or neglect *before* the birth of her child is a fairly recent phenomenon.

For those who believe that a fetus is a person from the moment of conception, the argument of privacy in pregnancy has fewer complex meanings, but for the majority of people who are not willing to attest to the exact moment that a fetus becomes a human being, endowed with the same rights as those of us who walk the earth unaided by umbilical cord, the terrain known as "fetal care/fetal neglect" raises shocking and disturbing questions about government control and about invasion by others. In the summer of 1989 the Reproductive Rights Project of the American Civil Liberties Union (ACLU) reported that they were seeing fetal neglect and fetal abuse charges on a regular basis, often a few a week.

It was a California case in 1986, however, that brought the issue of fetal neglect to light and illustrated the vulnerability of poor women. A San Diego resident, Pamela Rae Stewart Monson, was charged with *criminal negligence* because she gave birth to a "brain-dead" infant son, who died three months later. According to the prosecution, the child's condition and subsequent death was a result of the mother's "fetal neglect." The seeming precedent and validity for such cases stem from the existence of a variety of state "feticide" laws that permit prosecution for murder when a fetus is killed during a fatal or near-fatal attack of a pregnant woman (e.g., the ghastly murder of the actress Sharon Tate, then pregnant, at the hands of Charles Manson's gang). As we have seen time and again, whatever the motivating incident may be for the enactment of a law, any group can come to hail it as their own if they can make it work for their ends. In this case, the existence of "feticide" laws provides the right-to-life movement with a legal foundation for the persecution and prosecution of women.

The Monson infant presumably had barbiturates and amphetamines in his blood. In the lawsuit filed against Mrs. Monson, it was alleged that she had been warned not to take drugs, not to have intercourse, and to seek medical attention immediately if she began to hemorrhage. According to the prosecution, she failed to behave in a manner that would have provided the maximum safety for her unborn child. Monson did not receive any prenatal medical care until the seventh month of her pregnancy.

Underlying the Monson case is the question of social class in America. The quality and availability of prenatal care for poor women are seriously lacking in our country. It is wrong to assume that poor women are not motivated to take care of themselves during pregnancy and then of their babies. It is, instead, the reality of their poverty and the absence of consistently good prenatal care that prevent many from acting in ways we have come to define as responsible mothering. However the feticide laws came into existence, once established they lay a strong foundation for the bricks of a fetal-rights wall. Most important, underpinning the notions of fetal care, fetal neglect, fetal responsibility, is the public regulation of pregnancy. Many babies have been born damaged or dead in past decades, and centuries because of the mother's bad habits or the neglect of her body, whether willful, or out of ignorance, poverty, or substance addiction. With the advent of fetal-neglect cases, and based on feticide laws, the privacy of pregnancy is further violated. This precedent could be used for the employment of a series of public policies that would monitor and control pregnant citizens. Smoking is only one example of a private behavior known to be unhealthy to a fetus; the consumption of alcohol, another known detriment to the unborn, and the widespread and growing use of other drugs are the most striking dangers to the unborn.

Presumably well-meaning health advocates could run afoul of privacy in pregnancy. Two physicians in Parkside, a suburb of Philadelphia, offered an inducement to pregnant women. As obstetricians, they provided $100 discounts to pregnant women who quit smoking. They were physicians who had observed the differences in the health of smoking and nonsmoking women and their delivered babies, and their intentions were probably all to the good of the mothers and the babies. Yet there is a darker side to their inducement that makes it substantially different from the discounts offered to nonsmokers by health or life insurance companies. In the case of the insurance rates, the person involved is responsible only for him- or herself; choose to smoke or choose to quit. In the case of the doctors, the discount offered was based on medical research that points to healthier babies being born to women who do not smoke. Does it then follow that expectant mothers should be monitored to be sure that their behavior or habits do not harm the fetuses they are carrying? Which is the more important value to our society: to safeguard the individual privacy of pregnant women, or to ensure the society of healthier, chubbier babies—babies less likely to need state care or aid?

In fairness, the doctors in question did not pry into the lives of their patients; those women who chose to quit smoking were rewarded by a small discount in delivery costs. It does, however, provide a good introduction to the notion of fetal neglect. It raises the seemingly simple but desperately complex question: should privacy in pregnancy be protected even if it might mean that some babies will not be as healthy as other babies? And more importantly, whose responsibility is it to assure, to the extent possible, the delivery of healthy babies? Is it the responsibility of mature, responsible women (with the aid of their families and at the suggestions of their doctors), or is it the responsibility of law, public policy, or, in the extreme case, religious zealots who place the rights of the unborn above the rights of the living?

There is, I believe, a substantial difference between nutritional and educational programs and other forms of federal, state, and municipal aid available to impoverished women during their pregnancies and the demand that women behave in certain ways in order to protect their unborn. Yet it is also easy to understand how the water gets muddied once the state, or anyone other than the family, gets involved with the well-being of pregnant women. Liberal social welfare programs sponsored by those who are pro-choice might provide a kind of precedent for fetal-neglect cases, which are so popular among anti-abortion crusaders. Once the business of minding the health of pregnant women and their potential offspring is placed outside the purview of the family, then it becomes an ideological and privacy free-for-all, with each side choosing their weapons and shields. With the United States ranked an incredible nineteenth among industrialized nations in infant mortality rates, the questions must be posed—would less privacy in pregnancy cause fewer deaths of infants, and what loss of freedom would ensue? As women's rights advocates sadly saw, family policy issues were not theirs alone. Issues about the family were readily seized and distorted by opposing ideological forces. It is perhaps inescapable that in the attempt to provide assistance to pregnant women we open the door of opportunity to more control. If this is true, is the trade-off worth it, so that we might increase the rate of live and healthy infants? Government nutritional and prenatal programs suggest that we do believe that the life of the unborn is worthy of our public attention and care. Might we then also argue that a resulting invasion of privacy, while it might be unintentional, is not surprising?

When there is not a "perfect privacy" in pregnancy, that is, when privacy in pregnancy is not an absolute value, the argument centers on whose life and whose rights are paramount (mother or fetus). The promotion of civil liberties for the fetus are advocated by people who would not, on any other dimension, call themselves civil libertarians. The American Civil Liberties Union was unequivocal in their position on the California Monson case mentioned above—they held that a woman's privacy exceeded any claim of the state to have a stake in her pregnancy. In the tangle of fetal neglect we see the difficulty of compromise between those who adhere to a complete privacy sanction and those who lobby for the rights of the unborn.

Monson, the California woman, was charged under a law originally intended to force fathers of illegitimate children to support the women during pregnancy. According to the Reproductive Rights Project of the ACLU, the law was never intended to be used *against* women, but rather to be used *for women's protection and benefit*. The supposed benign regulation of pregnancy by law has been coopted by the interference of the political forces of the New Right and its allied groups. The inversion of protective legislation for women into a tool of discrimination is not new. We have seen the limiting effects of "protective" measures for women in employment practices for a very long time.

The delivery of social services to pregnant women poses a dilemma because it is at once both a form of protection for women and a form of invasion or intrusion, which can, when in the wrong hands, be most detrimental to women's rights. It is one thing to entrust a medical doctor with the power to help a woman decide on an abortion, but it paves the way for the kind of grotesque abuse evidenced in the Monson fetal-neglect case. This case, and those like it, invest in the doctor a kind of judicial and legal power, closer to tyranny than to the sage advice of a trusted family "medical friend." Instead it elevates medical opinion and counsel to law. It also suggests that the refusal to follow your doctor's advice, should he or she be of a different political stripe, might find you reported straightaway to the authorities. It changes the concept of following your doctor's advice for your own good to an injunction that you must follow your doctor's advice or face penalty of law.

A doctor might tell a middle-aged man to stop smoking. If he refuses and then dies of cardiac arrest from high blood pressure, or from smoking induced cancer, it is a tragedy for the man, his family, and his friends. It is not, however, something likely to motivate prosecution for not taking the doctor seriously. After all, who would one prosecute, the dead man? It is specifically the pregnant woman in our society, entrusted with the next generations, who is most vulnerable to this kind of invasion and intimidation. In other cases, the refusal of women to consent to cesarean section deliveries has prompted similar public and legal reactions from hospitals, doctors, and right-to-life advocates. In another case, a woman dying of cancer in a Washington, D.C., hospital was forced by a hospital-secured court order to undergo a cesarean section after her husband, her parents, and her personal physician said no. The infant died almost instantly, and the cancer-patient mother, within a few days. These incidents tell us that we are unclear about where responsibility, and final decision, rest with regard to the unborn. Much later, the District of Columbia Court of Appeals ruled that the operation had been in error of the law and should not have been performed.

Roe gave women, of the appropriate age and financial means, the ability to claim the guarantee of privacy in their decisions to terminate pregnancy. However, the existence of fetal neglect says that all women are potentially accountable for the outcome of their pregnancy and the condition of their offspring at birth. Although the Monson case in San Diego was eventually dismissed, it exists as a cold and stark reminder that privacy in pregnancy is at best an elusive goal. Does a pregnant woman have the right to exist in a vacuum with the full complement of her liberties protected, or does she, by virtue of her pregnancy, move into another class of citizen—a citizen whose obligations to society are such that her rights and liberties become secondary, or at worst, temporarily suspended?

State Neglect:
The Ultimate Betrayal

The state's tolerance of fetal-neglect lawsuits lends legitimacy to the claim for status for the unborn. As we have seen, people absolutely unrelated to families believe they should make decisions for fetuses and increasingly for comatose patients in cases involving the principle of the right to die. These right-to-life forces get appointed as guardians and argue always on the side of preserving "life" at any level and at any cost. These cases dramatically pit the woman against her fetus. Once the fetus is born, however, the state drops its "compelling interest in preserving life."

The United States is one of the richest countries in the world, yet we are cutting back on our welfare services to children and are still unable to come to grips with an almost Third World ranking in infant mortality. Yet many thousands of Americans can work up more than a little protective sympathy for fetuses and even for bunches of frozen cells. We are a country that cares little for babies once they are born and in dire need of assistance.

There are people, children and adults, that we, as a society, have deserted. Those citizens the civil rights activist and lawyer Roger Wilkins has termed the "throwaway people." American society tries to pretend that they are "out of sight and out of mind" and has cast them away as just so much unpleasant rubble.

These are most certainly people with a "right to life"— a right to live. But their concerns have been left traditionally to the "liberals," those, incidentally, who are also most likely to honor the right to reproductive choice and the right to die. What is the appeal for the right-to-life forces of the desperately damaged infant, the unformed fetus, and the comatose patient? Perhaps these forms of life are a much less threatening reality than the survival needs, tragic and compelling, of living, thinking, conscious, and fully formed children and adults in the worst poverty-stricken urban areas.

By and large, these people believe that the faceless tissue conglomeration, known medically as the zygote, is a life worth saving. What does their zealotry to save both the formless fetuses and the hapless souls in a vegetative state tell us about their priorities and their values as caring human beings?

Their energies and concerns are certainly more urgently needed to nurture and enrich the lives of those children already born and those adults who have their mental functioning intact. Many infants are thrust into the agony invariably accompanying poverty in our urban ghettoes. Children raising children, born into single-parent homes, where our infant mortality rate is higher than in any other industrial society. Hundreds of thousands of able-bodied adults, uneducated, with little hope for a decent life, drifting without marketable job skills, are unable to find work other than in the most menial jobs invariably paying the minimum hourly wage, and sometimes less.

It is, however, far too simplistic to assert that any and all intrusion can only be onerous or evil. Laws that sought to protect women from brutal attacks, which in turn might harm their pregnancies, were originally well intentioned. The doctors who wanted their pregnant patients to stop smoking were probably equally well intentioned. Certainly, programs monitoring a poor pregnant woman's nutritional needs are based on a humanitarian perspective. Yet from there we move to the reality of addicted women giving birth to addicted babies and to desperately ill, AIDS-infected babies, and we are forced to ask: what should we as a society do about the well-being of our infants, if it requires intervention *before* they actually become infants?

We are left wondering whether the well-intentioned care of the pregnant woman can ever be separated from the intrusion of the fetal-rights groups. Perhaps most crucially, can we disentangle all of this from the frightening distinctions by class and race that are raised by intervention?

The mixture of pregnancy with addiction or serious drug use is sobering. A 1988 national hospital survey found that at least 11 percent of the women surveyed had used illegal drugs during their pregnancies. Whether these particular statistics are reliable enough for us to make generalizations is beyond the scope of this essay. What remains for our consideration is the undeniable reality of babies born, many thousands each year, who suffer, from the very moment of their birth, from serious health damage due to the drug use of their mothers.

On one level we might justifiably ask what kind of a callous society says "Too bad, these innocent infants will have to suffer because we must not monitor the behavior or intervene in the lives of the individual mothers. You, little one, are entering this world without much of a chance because we protected your mother's rights." This is, of course, precisely the kind of sentiment utilized by the pro-life groups who believe that the fetus is a full-blown human life, that civil liberties begin in the womb, and that there is nothing fundamentally frightening or dangerous about the wholesale monitoring of pregnant women through state or federally controlled programs. Further pain is added to this already tragic scenario because so few drug rehabilitation centers or detox clinics are willing to take pregnant women due to liability and insurance problems. Thus the high-risk pregnant, poor, and drug-abusing woman, hoping to break her drug habit of her own volition to protect her fetus, usually finds no welcome in governmentally run subsidized detox programs.

Is there a way to get away from a "1984" spectre of millions of pregnant women lined up to get their blood and urine tested at neighborhood or community "pregnancy monitoring centers," probably handily renamed something euphemistic such as "maternal health centers"? This is all too reminiscent of the extreme population control program of "one child per family" in the People's Republic of China, where women of childbearing age have their menstrual cycles monitored monthly by the state. A failure to report can bring out the authorities to ensure that the absent Chinese woman is not pregnant with a second child. Measures of control over individual life in an area as intuitively private as pregnancy makes the American democrat in most of us shudder. There is now a medical technique known as radioimmunoassay, which enables traces of cocaine to be detected by analyzing a few strands of hair.

If a society chooses to rationalize the invasion of privacy in order to help ensure the health of its future generations, then it can also move to a rationalization of pregnancy monitoring, which would, over time (and maybe in a comparatively short time, given the economic and political pressures to do so), redefine and extend the meaning of "high-risk pregnancy." Sick women, women with kidney disease, arthritis, diabetes, the panoply of autoimmune connective tissue disorders such as lupus, and the virtually limitless array of diseases that have some hereditary factors, could all come under the category of "high risk."

Given the possibility of producing new generations of damaged children, those who continue to define privacy as the ultimate good might find themselves defined as the more callous. If we continue to mire ourselves in our traditional rights paradigm, those who protect privacy in pregnancy might look forward to a time when *they* will be seen as the evil side, and that those previously called callous and antagonistic to women, namely the New and Fundamentalist Right, might move into an arena where they are perceived as friends to women and to life. It is a bizarre ideological flim-flam game that we have perhaps reached, a place where those antagonists, who are the direct ancestors of the conservative social Darwinist view of human life, will claim humanitarian territory as rightfully their own. Haven't we as a society crossed into a realm of crisis so intense and obvious, demanding that a new model must be created and employed that can honor both liberty and life?

It is the notion of the fetus as person that most complicates the issue. Until we find a way to protect unborn life without a complete disregard for the integrity of the life of the already existing woman, we will run eternally into the wall of privacy and will find many casualities as a result. The very notion of "welfare of the mother" programs being taken over by right-wing forces under the banner of pregnancy monitoring places us in an irreconcilable conflict with liberty and the well-being of society. While these values have often been at swords' points with one another, rarely have we witnessed this democratic trade-off in a more tragic and dramatic duel. The sure losers of this conflict are women. While all conflicts between individual freedoms and the "public good" pose problems for a society with a structure such as ours, it is in the area of pregnancy where the contradiction applies to women only. This forces us to consider the grave effects it may ultimately have on a woman's status in the society and on her very claim to citizenship.

The apparently increasing trend of drug abuse among pregnant women is particularly sorrowful, because once again it places the poor and pregnant woman at the most fragile and marginal edge of existence. Despite reports that drug abuse is no longer completely isolated in the poor or the minority communities, it is poverty that more than any other factor precludes privacy. It is the poor, drug-abusing pregnant woman most likely to be turned away from a public detox program, most likely to be monitored, and most likely to be unable to escape the monitoring if such programs were to be instituted at a national level. The Southern Poverty Law Center, in its work on justice in the South, continues to see the involuntary sterilization of poor women as a major issue of discrimination and injustice. What better solution to these high-risk, drug-using, AIDS carrying women of childbearing age than forced sterilization?

The amount of public attention paid to women as mothers is particularly ironic, since this attention is primarily due to the velocity of the abortion issue and the tireless fight waged by abortion's opponents. Yet the emphasis on abortion, and by extension on motherhood, puts women back in a nineteenth- or, at best, early-twentieth-century framework. This model makes motherhood a woman's chief or primary occupation or, at least, preoccupation. Women as the primary caregivers in society is a topic for another book, and many scholars have dealt with it. However, child care, pregnancy, and the attendant cares of bringing up the next generations cannot be only women's issues or feminist issues. They are human issues. It is not until they are moved from an exclusively female arena that women will also move away from an arena where they come under such intensive attack. To honor the sanctity of fetal life while government and its policies ignore the needs of the precious lives of already born children constitutes a kind of national betrayal.

A Woman Called Jane, a Baby Named Louise

A little more than a decade ago a baby girl named Louise Brown was born in the United Kingdom. Her birth heralded the beginning of the era of reproductive technology. "Conceived" in a laboratory, she was known in the press at the time as the "test-tube baby" or the "petri-dish infant." The birth of Louise Brown also concluded another era by signifying, in a recorded way, the end of the automatic expectation of privacy in pregnancy. The context of her existence (or preexistence) foreclosed the mystery of pregnancy and in some basic way forever altered the definition of pregnancy itself. The way that Louise Brown came to be a human being marked her as a unique infant. More critically, her successful birth as the result of a technologically aided conception gave her a special status that contributed a significant link to the increasingly bitter fight about the status of the unborn.

Perhaps we should have been wiser when Louise Brown was born and immediately recognized that her birth was not a one-in-a-million occurrence. It would have been prudent to acknowledge that reproductive science was not going to stop at the petri-dish level of invention and sophistication, and to realize that neither our ethical standards nor our legal codes were up to what would all too soon be required of them. Today's new pregnancy and birth technologies so completely revamp our notions of pregnancy and childbirth that if our public policies do not soon keep pace with this new world, high technology will rule over ethics, integrity, and privacy.

Precisely because of the multiplying and changing technological advances, an ethics for this modern age must be found. Nowhere is it more evident than in our medical techniques used at both the beginning and the ending of life. Many of the same ethical and policy dilemmas present in birth decisions confront us at the end of life. We increasingly seem to believe that to accept death at virtually any point in the life cycle is to fall prey to some sort of antilife phobia (witness the amount of medical technology and research devoted to sustaining life far beyond its natural or meaningful course). The questions about privacy in death will be discussed later, but it is worth mentioning here that the connection between birth and death has never been more profound or ironic than in our present age. Technology has merged life with death in a way not before experienced. Modern medicine has collapsed the concept of "real time" in the life span.

The language of the judicial opinion in the Davis case of the frozen zygotes, the emotional intensity surrounding cases of fetal neglect, the Pandora's box of surrogate arrangements, the intrusion of unknown and unfriendly "guardians"—all of these elements are mirrored in the abortion debate itself. These are circumstances and events which vividly connect a plaintiff called Jane Roe to a baby named Louise Brown.

Part Three
Hearts and Souls:
A Privacy Metaphor

AIDS:

Privacy's New Prism

I have taken on a grisly habit; I read the obituaries in the *New York Times* every morning. I read to see how many men under the age of fifty have died. Then I continue with a macabre checklist: Was AIDS actually listed as the cause of death? Did the name of a same-gender "companion" appear as survivor? Was there a surviving wife listed, surviving children? Does the obituary say "respiratory failure" or "pneumonia?" Are these euphemisms for AIDS? Then I speculate, how did the families choose to include or exclude items that would lead the way not just to the cause of death but to gossip, speculation, and conclusions about the style and course of the deceased's life?

On January 23, 1989, the *New York Times* published the following obituary, written by reporter Woody Hochswender:

John Duka, 39, Former *Times* Writer on Fashion and Art.

99

> John Duka, a journalist who wrote with humor and
> grace about fashion, art, and society, died Saturday
> morning at his Manhattan home. He was 39 years old.
> His wife, Kezia Keeble Duka, said Mr. Duka died of com-
> plications stemming from major abdominal surgery in
> November. He was diagnosed as having acquired im-
> mune deficiency syndrome a year ago, she said.…
> Besides his wife he is survived by his mother, brother,
> and his twin sister.

From the above obituary the average reader could
deduce anything we choose to about the marriage, the
private life of the deceased. We might try to put together
the pieces of a married couple's perhaps agonizing personal puzzle; we might be right, we might be wrong.
Almost certainly, it is none of our business! Perhaps we
should not be offered information to use as tools in
armchair sleuthing exercises into a family's life and its
sorrows. Yet that obituary, and many more just like it
during these AIDS years, suggests it is our business. The
speculation and questioning that occur are an inevitable,
if inadvertent, consequence of revealing the cause of
death when that cause is this loaded and pejorative illness called AIDS.

Do these obituaries tell us too much? Sometimes I
think we have taken on a kind of fascination with the
numbers falling from this plague. There is a "Typhoid
Mary was here" death rhetoric in the air. Are we more fas-
cinated with the exposure of a person's sexuality than we
are struck with the horror of the countless dead? For

some families the experience and revelation of a death from AIDS is a terrible humiliation. For others it is the death of the loved one that is the overwhelming sorrow, the cause of death secondary. In the case of Michael Bennett, the choreographer and playwright who brought us *A Chorus Line*, or the fashion designer Perry Ellis, or the artist Robert Mapplethorpe or the renowned choreographer Robert Joffrey, and countless others just as famous, AIDS probably could not have been hidden.

Once articulated, AIDS is the pebble in the lake causing ripple after ripple of privacy invasion. Susan Sontag has argued that the demystification of cancer has been beneficial for those with the disease. The "defanging" of the word *cancer* has helped those suffering from it; but the label AIDS has very long and far-reaching fangs. It is not clear how much directness and revelation benefits those involved.

Talk about sexuality and privacy has become more complicated. Now thoughts about sexuality, disclosure, and privacy are filtered through the reality of AIDS. *AIDS* has become the inevitable next word when we say *homosexuality . . . sexuality . . . privacy*. AIDS is a prism for our human tragedy. It is virtually impossible to talk or write about privacy and sexuality without, in the same breath, announcing the presence of AIDS, accounting for it somehow. To do otherwise at the present moment in our society risks one's credibility. We must, however, suspend our disbelief for a moment and pretend that the AIDS crisis is over, a part of recorded history, as is the record of the widespread horrors of the bubonic plague in

Europe or the true story of Typhoid Mary in America.

This fantasy exercise has a point. Long after its cure, AIDS will stand as the leitmotif of privacy's dilemmas. The presence of AIDS in many ways serves as privacy's minefield. Its spectre and its dread compel us to confront, all at once, and around one issue, privacy risks and outcomes. The many themes and contradictions of privacy are found here in the AIDS drama ... privacy and the public good ... privacy and sexuality ... death ... liability ... freedom ... control ... danger. There are few questions about private and public distinctions not represented somewhere in the AIDS experience. I do not intend to make light of a far-reaching health disaster by simply reducing it to a useful paradigm for social analysis. We can, however, consider that within this terrible tragedy, privacy's largely unresolved elements are played out. They are played out in ways forcing us to confront why we have not established the fundamental borders of this liberty's terrain.

Someone to Blame

For centuries, homosexuals have been vulnerable to attack and have provided numerous societies with a ready-made class of scapegoats. The originating incidence of AIDS in the homosexual population allows us to lay at the feet of that community the blame for much of what we do not understand about disease, sexuality, or how to protect privacy during a state of crisis.

Whether AIDS began in Africa or Haiti as a generalized and random disease largely occurring among heterosexuals no longer matters. In the United States it originated in the homosexual community. We must honestly confront that reality and understand that all of our talk about the increased incidence in heterosexual communities, drug-using communities, and poverty-stricken communities does not erase the memory of where AIDS began. It began among a group already considered by many to be "unclean" and suspect. AIDS provided a marvelous opportunity to justify the exclusion of a group many find offensive to begin with, and to further delay a serious discussion about their entitlement to civil liberties. After all, we are bracing ourselves for a national health disaster with staggering economic and social consequences, and the originating "culprits" are the sexually nonconforming!

Finding a prompt cure for AIDS is critical, but it will not cure the inescapable: that we find it easier to condone the invasion of the privacy of those we disapprove of than those we see as part of the mainstream. Now we have the ability to create, with adequate rationales, however morally indefensible, a true leper or untouchable class. AIDS screams "fragility" at us at a time when our nation, thanks largely to the legacy of eight years of President Reagan's sermonic exhortations, had begun to believe that we were nearly invincible. Scourges and plagues belonged to a "lesser" people of another time, precivilizations that did not know about hygiene, antibiotics, and miracle drugs. Plagues belonged to barbarians or weaker and poorer cultures—a disease that can fell a civilization or many of its members could not happen to us; we had moved beyond that.

Never mind that the course of human history is a chronicle, in part, of enormous devastation due to illness. No, we are above all that. This is the modern age. We have had the war on poverty; the war on crime; the war on cancer; the war on drugs. (We haven't won these wars, but the rhetoric does not allude to that fact.) We have raced to the moon and back and sent our spaceships to Neptune. We are angry at homosexuals because they are ruining our plan for immortality and permanent victory against human frailty.

If we cannot cure it, we ought to at least be able to blame it on someone or some group. It is best and ever so handy if we can blame it on those citizens we can easily slip into the classification of "other"—"not like me." For many, homosexuals are an adequate pariah group, but even the homophobic can work up a bit of sympathy for the young and talented dropping in such numbers. As AIDS increasingly moves into the poor, minority, and marginal communities, hastened by the drug disaster in our inner cities, one shudders to think of the implications. In his book *Shattered Mirrors*, Monroe Price has said: "AIDS has been a plague of blame and fear. It now promises to be a plague of unfairness, indifference and discrimination."

In her work on the origins of blame, Dorothy Nelkin

has traced the history of disease and the faces of blame. People in societies afflicted with serious waves of illness or plague have always tried to disassociate themselves from those perceived to be the "carriers." The fault traditionally has been laid at the feet of those easily identifiable as "other"—foreigners; those with nonconforming behaviors; and now, finally, those whose lifestyles are seen to have put them, and the larger society, at risk.

Sontag writes, in both her early work *Illness as Metaphor* and in her newer work *AIDS and Its Metaphors*, about the power of a disease's label. In tuberculosis, in cancer, and now in AIDS, those infected are seen as unclean and as shamed in some significant way. With AIDS this is especially so. As Sontag says: "It is not a mysterious affliction that seems to strike at random. Indeed, to get AIDS is precisely to be revealed, in the majority of cases so far, as a member of a certain 'risk group,' a community of pariahs" (*AIDS and Its Metaphors*, pp. 24–25). AIDS is a fearful and vibrant reminder of the power a disease can have to destroy the fabric of a person's life.

Not so long ago we did not speak the name of cancer in its full syllabic content. I am poignantly reminded of this whenever I talk to people of my parent's generation—an eighty-year-old friend always says that his wife died of "The Big C." Sontag writes of our new openness about disease in the following way:

> The word cancer is uttered more freely and people are not often described anymore in obituaries as dying of a

"very long illness." ... The new candor about cancer is part of the same obligatory candor (or lack of decorum) that brings us diagrams of the rectal-colon or genito-urinary tract ailments of our national leaders on television and on the front pages of newspapers—more and more it is precisely a virtue in our society to speak of what is supposed *not* to be named. The change can also be explained by the doctors' fear of lawsuits in a litigious society.

I am not persuaded that the reason for the revelatory medical rhetoric stems causally or directly from the medical profession's fear of malpractice lawsuits. In any event, that is not the issue considered here. Sontag's point is correct. We are much more open about disease and illness. Why have we come to believe that it is somehow appropriate, much less obligatory, to discuss and show such matters in the national media?

There is a worrisome price connected to this openness. We can argue that to list AIDS directly and publicly as the cause of death is an attempt to detoxify it and lessen its impact and the resultant prejudice. It might be a brave decision on the part of a particular family; but I doubt that holding one's head up high and proclaiming the presence of AIDS does much to elicit sympathy or reduce terror among those who still see it as evidence of dangerous morals and a sinful life.

Rock Hudson's Own "Pillow Talk":
The Multiple Binds of the Public/Private Gay Man

> "Just make sure you do plenty of scoring out there."
> "I'll do my best." —*Rock Hudson*
> (*from the 1959 romantic comedy* Pillow Talk,
> *also starring Doris Day and Tony Randall*)

The movie star Rock Hudson was a victim of AIDS, and at the time of his death perhaps its most publicized. Always the perfect, if somewhat cardboard, leading man, he played the most eligible bachelor around. Whatever his screen portrayals, Hudson's heart beat to the homosexual drummer of love. Yet his homosexuality was virtually unknown outside the movie industry. When the news spread that he was being treated in the experimental AIDS program in Paris, it was headlined in newspapers around the world. The report was doubly newsworthy: the illness itself, and the ever-present factor of "Aha! Another closet homosexual found out!" Hudson's death is a story of deception, betrayal, and a tortured attempt to keep a life private against all odds. The aftermath of his death involved a lawsuit against his estate by a former lover. AIDS precluded Hudson from having much dignity during his last days. The attention his affliction received was a reminder of just how far-reaching an effect AIDS can have on individuals and on our legal, moral, journalistic, and ethical standards.

Hollywood is a funny place, filled with open sexuality and fault-free adultery—yet to this day the industry does not embrace nor does it expose either the male or female homosexuality of its stars. The *Variety* reporter who exposed Hudson's illness initially was thought by many in the industry to have betrayed a confidence, not just of Hudson's but of the larger community's. Hudson may have chosen to keep his lifestyle quiet primarily for his survival as a star. Even today it is most unlikely that an open homosexual in American films would win favor as a leading man, but public disclosure, ought, in any case, to rest with the individual involved.

The attorneys for Marc Christian, Rock Hudson's lover, claimed that the movie star's medical condition had been hidden from Mr. Christian. According to the allegations of the lawsuit, Hudson demanded that his staff keep his illness secret until almost his dying day. In a much-disputed quotation, Rock Hudson's secretary is alleged to have said: "Rock told me: 'Take care of the kid. I may have killed him.'" The secretary, Mark Miller, and Hudson's estate claimed just the opposite. They said that Hudson had ended his relationship with Christian on a bitter note because of Christian's promiscuity. In yet another layer of alleged betrayal, the lawyers for Hudson's estate argue that the reason Hudson allowed his former lover to continue living in his home was because Christian had threatened to expose Hudson as an active homosexual, and that one of Christian's threats was to release Hudson's homosexual love letters to the press.

Did Hudson know about his illness early on, and did he fail to tell his lover for reasons of vanity or insecurity? Did Hudson believe that Christian had given him AIDS, and therefore did not feel any responsibility toward him? Or was it true, as the lover alleged in his suit, that he was the victim of betrayal, and that he had the absolute right to know immediately that Hudson was infected with, and indeed dying of, AIDS? What rights should a nondisclosed or "closet" homosexual have in keeping secret his identity? Should it even include his infection with the disease so linked with homosexuality and death? These are questions that torture every relationship where there is any chance of being exposed to the HIV virus.

Is there ever an excuse or a justification for keeping secret from one's lover the knowledge that one is carrying AIDS or is infected? When the result of being ill from AIDS is so uniformly fatal, it is hard to imagine a time when silence is appropriate. Common decency, humanity, loyalty, to say nothing of love or affection, dictate prompt and total revelation. Yet it is naive to assume that all people want to or feel they can be completely up-front in their sexual encounters.

The jury in the Hudson case decided they understood the price of privacy in this instance. Marc Christian, four years after the fact, and still HIV *negative*, was awarded more money than the sum total of the Hudson estate. The jury's first award was $7.25 million; they then came

109

back with an additional $14.5 million for "punitive" damages. They, the jury, found Rock Hudson's behavior "outrageous." Perhaps what they really found outrageous was his homosexuality; how dare he live this paradoxical "fake" life—the dashing heterosexual man-about-town on the screen, and the private homosexual.

Gay rights groups, including the well-established and respected Lambda Legal Defense and Education Fund, found this judgment particularly disturbing for the larger gay community. They and other civil liberties groups perceived the massive size of the judgment as a symbolic punitive judgment against homosexuality itself. It is hardly an original thought to suggest that in the mid-1980s, a time forever altered by the reality of AIDS, a young man, not brain-damaged, living in the sophisticated glitter of Los Angeles, who was engaged in homosexual activities with someone considerably older who had lived a homosexual life for years, ought to think very soberly indeed about the kind of sex he is engaging in. And if he does not choose to do that, can the other partner be sued as though the acts in the bedroom were criminal ones? When Christian saw Hudson getting so frail, thinner, sicker, it is hard to take seriously his claim that he believed that Hudson was suffering from anorexia or skin cancer. Maybe the real secret to the public trial is the private anger and heartbreak that Marc Christian was excluded from Rock Hudson's will.

Anne Taylor Fleming, writing for the *New York Times*

on February 15, 1989, about the Hudson trial, il-luminated the confusions:

> On one level, the trial was darkly amusing—pin-striped establishment lawyers rattling off details of homosexual acts with unblushing exactitude, as if they discussed such things every day. There was something refreshing in the exercise: AIDS, it seems, has come even further out of the closet than many of us supposed. It is also salutary to be reminded that those who die of AIDS are not its only victims: there are the survivors too. But, of course, there is the flip side—privacy and love taken public. What right have any of us to turn the private tenderness of old lovers into public trash or to brand-ish their love letters in a court of law? And didn't Rock Hudson have the right to die the way he wanted, still in the shadows, his obituary to read "liver cancer" or one of those other euphemisms used to describe death by AIDS?

"HIV Positive"—Exposure, Then Expulsion!: The Gay Man as Leper

The words "HIV positive" have become synonymous with fear and dread. HIV is the virus name for what we call AIDS. Those who test positive for the HIV virus are assumed to be infected with the disease. But not all who test positive will be stricken with the full-blown and fatal version. To be HIV positive means that you are (a) a carrier and (b) at much greater risk than a person who is HIV negative. Although the test itself is a simple procedure, the ramifications are not.

When a contagious disease hits a group that happens also to be without any guaranteed civil rights as a group, a diagnostic tool, such as a blood test, can become a weapon of exposure and the harbinger of personal and professional demise, even if the individual is lucky enough not to die from the disease. The protection of privacy takes on a particular urgency when the group is one that has witnessed so much intolerance and persecution in the past even before the time they could be linked to causing any harm.

Some argue that we are in a national medical crisis, a disease without a cure continues to strike, a contagious disease transmitted from human to human, largely through sexual encounter or drug use. It is not illogical to reason further that anyone at risk should be "tagged" and tested accordingly. Even if we could be sure that the test itself was 100 percent fool-proof, required testing would still be a deadly trade-off in a democracy. The testing is not totally fool-proof; people can still test "false positive" due to a number of contaminating influences, including the presence of non-AIDS-related autoimmune disease.

Because this dread disease is so inextricably linked with sexual conduct, it is precluded from being as much in the open as it needs to be in order to stop its spread. Individuals in their intimate dealings ought to choose to tell the truth, but some do not. Can a society then inter-vene, to ensure that the *truth* will be told? And decide to whom, and for what purpose?

All homosexuals, indeed even those suspected of being homosexuals, could be rounded up and tested, with drug users and other at-risk groups right behind the gays. This testing conceivably could then lead to the "yellow star," not of Jewish identification, but the mark of the "plague carrier." However frightening it may be for the well-being of the body politic to rely on the integrity of individual citizens in their bedrooms, it is arguably less terrifying than the above scenario.

This is more than a hyperbolic speculation. In the win-ter of 1989–1990, the new commissioner of health for New York City took his post with the announced convic-tion that the quarantine of some AIDS patients or suf-ferers was called for in this crisis.

A number of distinguished medical professionals I spoke to voiced their concern about the dilemma of AIDS. One doctor I spoke to, who defines himself as both a liberal and a "staunch civil libertarian," nonetheless said to me: "In the next decades we will look back on this non-sense about not testing people for HIV [the AIDS virus] and ask where the hell our heads were. If it all comes out okay, fine. If it doesn't we are going to have paid a terrible price for having watched a society decline in numbers and in health because we had some misguided notion about freedom and liberty."

Many other self-defined civil libertarian medical people have confided to me their conundrum. On the one hand they want to protect the integrity of medical confidentiality. They do not want to aid in the creation of a medical "leper" class in the closing days of the twentieth century. They are defenders of liberty and individual privacy. On the other hand, doctors, as the guardians of the future, want to stem the tide of AIDS and to use to its best advantage the technology available that might help, including sophisticated diagnostic tools.

The point is rather more straightforward than we may be willing to face. Doctors should not be forced to be the guardians of our liberties. Liberty should be secured first, built on a bedrock foundation on which we continue to construct the appropriate public health policies, even in a time of grave crisis or threat, without the constant fear that to do so might foreshadow a kind of Nisei camp or leper colony isolation for certain citizens.

Plague Medicine and the Health of Civil Liberties

> "Plague is a convergence of disease and circumstance in a way that yields substantial change in a community."
> *Monroe Price*, Shattered Mirrors: Our Search for Identity and Community in the AIDS Era

In a shocking retreat from the hallowed notion of medical confidentiality, the American Medical Association (AMA) in July 1988 at its annual meeting in Chicago dealt with AIDS in the following way: They [the AMA] "strongly urged physicians to warn the sexual partners of patients found to carry the AIDS virus if there was no other way to alert them to the danger." While the doctors said that every attempt should be made to honor patient confidentiality, if an AIDS-infected patient continued to refuse to tell his sexual partner or partners the doctor had a duty to so inform those people.

What is startling about the AMA position, and has been pointed to by journalists and by gay activists, is that the AMA, through this position, opens the way, indeed, provides a kind of precedent, for doctors to be sued for nondisclosure of their patients' AIDS. Even before the AMA announcement, Rock Hudson's doctor was named in the lawsuit exactly on this issue: for the failure to breach the vow of confidentiality between doctor and patient. The Hippocratic oath, for centuries the ethical standard of medical practice, sounds a particular and shrill warning: "Whatever in connection with my professional practice or not in connection with it I may see or hear in the lives of men which ought not to be spoken abroad I will not divulge, as reckoning that all such should be kept secret."

One wonders how the physician would be able to discover the identity of all the sexual partners of an infected patient who has no intention of notifying his partners . . . to say nothing of potential future partners. The AIDS epidemic was so threatening that the AMA stated that "it warranted an exception to the Hippocratic oath. . . . " The

AMA also stated that they felt that the primary obligation for control of the disease rested with the state and federal public health agencies. The precedent to the infringement of privacy is clear in this AMA posture, but even if the civil liberties implications were not so terrifying, the strategy is, on its face, a fairly feeble attempt aimed at controlling the spread of AIDS.

There is a more intimate and personal issue involved in AIDS, and that is the right to keep knowledge from oneself, in other words, to keep a secret from yourself. There are many gay men who had numerous sexual partners in the halycon days of liberated sex in baths and elsewhere. Some of them know that they are carriers because they have been tested; miraculously, others have tested negative despite the deaths of their lovers.

Some have died over the course of the last years knowing, and some not knowing, the results of the tests. Others have decided that there is no point in knowing. As one friend often says, "Why bother? If I know, it is a death sentence, a diagnostic death-test. It would make me crazy to know I had it, and I would keep waiting for the boom to be lowered. If I knew I was HIV negative, I would be sure that it was a mistake or just hadn't shown up yet."

Individual psychological makeup determines whether it makes a person "crazier" to know or not know if he or she carries the virus factor. Up until now, that has remained a choice individuals make for themselves. It is the decision to keep something private even from yourself. Given the spread of AIDS, can a person continue to claim that as a legitimate right? And if it is a right, is it morally correct to do so? When a society operates its supposed civil libertarian and democratic system in an exclusionary and nonegalitarian way, good people, moral people, may find themselves making self-protective decisions that are dissonant with their own ethical values in order to protect themselves. We are failing at something even broader and more important than finding the cure for AIDS when otherwise responsible citizens are put into this kind of a decision box.

Five years after the introduction of the HIV test, leading gay men's groups began to endorse voluntary, individual testing. The Gay Men's Health Crisis (GMHC), one of the most active and most vocal opponents of testing, reversed their position in the summer of 1989. Underscoring the above comments, the head of the organization said, "There are compelling reasons to get tested." Stressing the increasing legal protections of confidentiality and antidiscrimination measures and the hopeful signs seen from use of the drug AZT, the GMHC recommends testing because they see the results as somewhat less of a threat to the psychological and actual well-being of gay men. Yet it is critical to understand the context in which the testing has been placed by the GMHC. It is to be an individual, absolutely private and anonymous act and their informational campaign about the availability of the test stops far short of saying everyone who might be at risk should have it. Again, in the words of Richard Dunne, director of GMHC, "We have always felt that testing should be an individual decision.... Knowing one's test result is very powerful and some may not be able to handle it."

The response of the New York City health establishment helps illuminate the conflict between gay rights and the perceived public good. The then city's health commissioner, Dr. Stephen C. Joseph, while complimenting the gay community for moving so far from their previous position, nonetheless said, "It doesn't go far enough." Far enough would be that "the names of infected people tested through physicians, clinics, and hospitals would be confidentially reported to the Health Department for tracing of their sexual and needle-sharing drug contacts." The GMHC and other such organizations throughout the nation are vehemently opposed to any system of reporting, identification, or contact tracking.

The AIDS epidemic reminds us anew of our fears and prejudices. The strategy of "going public to become private" is particularly problematic for gays. This paradoxical position presents us with problems that have no easy panaceas or proven models for resolution. The AIDS epidemic makes the homosexual population ever more vulnerable, of that there is no doubt, but might this terror propel us to develop a new privacy model? One with a status and a set of rules that would work "in peacetime and in war"?

For those of us who are worried about civil liberties, the conflicted feelings about AIDS testing would be greatly diminished if we felt certain that those tested had some place to go for protection—if we felt that a systematic avenue of redress or recourse existed for those individuals suffering any abuses or unfair outcomes from the testing. Homosexuals are put into a kind of double jeopardy—first the exposure as homosexual, and then the discrimination if they are found to be suffering from the disease or discovered to be carriers of it. It is unfortunate that in our hurry to label homosexuality as perverse, unnatural, and unprotected, as a society we did not also consider that it is far easier to intervene actively in public health matters when all citizens are protected equally.

Was the threat to privacy inevitable with the advent of AIDS? The status of privacy is ambiguous in all instances, but during times of stress and emergency we are all the more vulnerable. Everything about the AIDS epidemic shows us that we must come to grips with the ways in which privacy fits into and significantly defines our notion of what really comprises the public good. There is a natural and healthy tension between freedom and control in a democratic society. It is not productive, however, for a society to be forced into making a trade-off between liberty or life, in its literal sense. That constitutes a value conflict healthy neither for the continuation of a people nor for the constitutional guarantees of equality.

The Paradox of
the Open Bedroom

The Public Stand for
Private Rights

The spring of 1986 was filled with protest, with hope, and with mobilization efforts for gay rights. Gay people had been fighting to achieve legal protection for their status long before 1986. That particular spring, however, was a critical juncture in the struggle for gay rights. Both lesbian and gay male activists were guarded, but hopeful; they felt it might be the year the legal tide would turn their way. That summer the Supreme Court would decide whether gay citizens had the right to engage in private homosexual acts, and whether that right was guaranteed to them through the auspices of the U.S. Constitution. The case, known as *Hardwick*, originated in Georgia and was brought to the Supreme Court as a case involving a Georgia man who claimed his privacy rights had been violated when he was arrested in his home during sexual intercourse with another man. If decided in the affirmative, it would be a landmark victory for homosexuals. Privately, some activists said that if the decision did go their way it could be as important to gay rights as the historic *Roe v. Wade* abortion decision had been to women's rights.

I witnessed a large protest march for gay rights during that spring. The mood of the participants was exuberant, enthusiastic, urgent. Many carried placards that stated their sexual preference as a public announcement of social status: "I Am Gay and Proud of It." Some carried signs that stated their relationship to a homosexual: "Proud Parent of a Gay Daughter/Son." Other marchers held signs that were political exhortations to action: "Join in the Fight for Rights for All People, Including Gays" or "Gays Deserve Constitutional Protection." There were a few young children marching with their homosexual fathers and lesbian mothers. I recall a little girl who carried a sign that read "I Love My Gay Dad."

I was deeply moved by this political demonstration, by the courage of those marching. I wondered if the Supreme Court would, in the final analysis, recognize the need for all its citizens to be covered by the great quilt of the U.S. Constitution. Despite that feeling, however, something inside me asked, "What's wrong here?" Memories of a "quiet time" classroom exercise from my earliest school days flooded into my mind, presented with a drawing captioned "What's wrong with this picture?" As school children we had to locate and circle the portion that did not belong or did not make sense. Something about the demonstration for gay rights did not make sense to me; I felt as if I had a puzzle before me and could not make all the pieces fit together correctly.

What was wrong with the picture of that spring day? These citizens were undeniably exercising their legitimate rights to speech, to protest, to assembly. Yet, there on the streets, they were also giving up a part of themselves, that most intimate, and in some ways most sacred, part of all humans. They were voluntarily revealing the identity of their sexual souls in the hope that they would come to a day when their private acts would be protected nationally by the power of the U.S. Constitution. "The love that dare not speak its name" was shouting its presence in broad daylight. This was not the same as a march for the right to vote or to engage in other public activities.

Taking to the streets to announce openly and publicly that most inherently private aspect of life—a person's bedroom behavior—they represented a striking paradox. The contradiction was that their protest actions were aimed at achieving recognition that gay *privacy* rights ought to be respected and legally guaranteed by the highest court in the land. Public demonstrations of gay pride (which are to some extent targeted at capturing heterosexual support) have stayed with me as a dramatic illustration of our muddle.

Between Consenting Adults . . .

However inherently private the bedroom might seem, the Supreme Court thought otherwise when it came to homosexual acts. The judgment went against Mr. Hardwick. The Court's written opinion invoked everything from the Bible to conventional notions of morality to prove the point that the gay population could not rely on a protective guarantee of privacy.

Justice Blackmun disagreed profoundly with the majority's attempt to define *Hardwick* as encompassing only the issue of the protection of sodomy. He said:

> This case is no more about a "fundamental right to engage in homosexual sodomy," as the court purports to declare, than *Stanley v. Georgia* (1969) was about a fundamental right to watch obscene movies, or *Katz v. United States* (1967) was about a fundamental right to place interstate bets from a telephone booth. Rather, this case is about "the most comprehensive of rights and the most valued by civilized men," namely, "the right to be let alone." (Justice Brandeis, 1928)

Justice Blackmun continued his dissent with a sharp disagreement with both the foundation and the tone of the majority decision when he stated:

> The assertion that "traditional Judeo-Christian values proscribe" the conduct involved, cannot provide an adequate justification.... That certain, but by no means all, religious groups condemn the behavior at issue gives the State no license to impose their judgments on the entire citizenry. The legitimacy of secular legislation depends on whether the State can advance some justification for its law beyond its conformity to religious doctrine.

124

Thus, far from buttressing his case, petitioner's invocation of Leviticus, Romans, St. Thomas Aquinas and sodomy's heretical status during the Middle Ages undermined his suggestion that section 16.6.2 represents a legitimate use of secular coercive power. A state can no more punish private behavior because of religious intolerance than it can punish such behavior because of racial animus.

Although the *Hardwick* decision in reality did little to alter daily life for most homosexuals, it was nonetheless a stunning defeat. It left gay activists and supporters no further opportunity to lull themselves into a sense of security under the delusion that the time had arrived when the law was on the side of a universal form of sexual liberty.

That decision illustrated vividly a complication: while sexual privacy might enjoy a kind of tacit approval among most Americans, and while it might be argued persuasively that all citizens ought to be entitled to this fundamental dignity, once you ask that the question be resolved officially, in a legal arena, you run the risk of learning that you are not entitled to any privacy at all. In this case, the prestigious and highly visible Supreme Court took the opportunity to reject the privacy claim of Mr. Hardwick, and to do so in a particularly punitive way. The gay rights strategy, which on the surface seemed logical and appropriate, proved a profound error, and, ironically, probably one that ultimately harmed their cause more than an affirmative decision might have helped it.

The gay rights movement had, mistakenly as it turned out, made a tactical decision to go forward with a claim under the entitlement of privacy. The continued existence of a number of arcane laws (largely unenforced) that prohibit certain sexual behaviors in a variety of states gave a kind of common sense logic to their approach. By the mid-1980s it might have seemed that our country had arrived at a place where all of its citizens had earned the entitlement to privacy in their bedrooms. The historic *Roe* decision added to the logic of a privacy precedent for previously taboo and illegal acts. The Supreme Court vehemently disagreed with this logic.

We are particularly confronted with the power of privacy's paradox in the homosexual case. Shouldn't gays be granted the dignity of bedroom privacy? If we say, resoundingly, *yes,* how do they then come back to ask for equal treatment before the law based on status and behaviors that were just defined as something beyond the scope of public purview? The answer could have rested with an affirmative decision in the *Hardwick* case; it did not. The road back to a campaign for public equality when you have sought, and lost, private sexual control is not one that may exist in any obvious way, at least at this time.

There are a myriad of rationales offered for the political strategy of the gay rights movement. Whatever the reluctance had been to wage the battle under equality claims, rather than under privacy ones, is somewhat irrelevant to the discussion at hand. Perhaps the pursuit of equality claims as a course of action seemed more risky, dangerous, and threatening than the course chosen.

Far after the fact, and long after his death, I realized that a dear family friend was probably homosexual. No one had discussed it. This adopted uncle, a product of his time, probably did not want his sexuality announced, nor would he have felt comfortable with an acknowledgment over the Thanksgiving turkey dinner. We were still in the closet as a society four decades ago. Most people were not interested in, or did not see a way to, express their sexuality, or much else. Matters of the heart and soul's yearnings were still private affairs.

Later in my life, living in the San Francisco Bay area during the first heady days of sexual freedom, experimentation, and the awakening of gay pride, "coming out" became a code of honor among many, but certainly not all, gay people. Bisexual and gay men who desired anonymity in their homosexual encounters frequented the bars and baths in San Francisco's gay neighborhood. The faceless sex of the homosexual bath assured gay men, especially those still in the closet, a kind of privacy. Use of the baths brought risks as well, not the least of which was the possibility of exposure in the most public way—police raids and arrest. The gay bathhouses, now of course long closed because of the AIDS epidemic, remain for me a metaphor of our confusion about the meaning of private acts.

Because gays have not been protected by the Constitution, they have done what most people would do: fought publicly and openly for their rights. Did Americans want to know so much about homosexuality? Or did the gay fight to gain recognition add to their vulnerability once AIDS hit? Awful and painful a question as it is to pose in a democracy, maybe, just maybe, because gays have been so proud, and so open, we are more discomforted about their existence, and a little more certain of their culpability in the AIDS crisis. As a society we do not yet know which parts of life we really want to have as routine, open matters of public discourse. But neither do we know with any certainty what we are willing to risk, or give up, or share, in order to provide people with the guarantees of privacy that might have kept them out of that very public light to begin with.

Pushed Out of the Closet: The Politics and Betrayals of "Outing"

> The message to rich and famous queers is: come out while you can, because when you die you'll be thrown on the cover of a magazine and labeled a closet case. I may even bring you out alive.—Michelangelo Signorile

Michelangelo Signorile has a cause; his mission is to reveal the homosexuality of other people. This practice has come to be known as "outing." Mr. Signorile is not a part of the New Right or the homophobic straight world;

he is a gay activist who believes that to be in the closet is to betray the cause of gay rights. At twenty-eight years of age, he is a product of the age of open gay pride. He assuredly is not a product of the fearful and restrictive days of past decades. Signorile came to the media's attention after the death of the multimillionaire and bon vivant Malcolm Forbes. As an editor of the gay activist magazine *Outweek*, he revealed Mr. Forbes as a deeply closeted homosexual, using the headline THE SECRET GAY LIFE OF MALCOLM FORBES with accompanying pictures that called into question Forbes's apparent heterosexuality.

Mr. Signorile and some of his colleagues believe that it is imperative that powerful people who are homosexuals announce themselves. They believe that these revelations will accomplish a number of things, chief among them being the recognition that homosexuality occurs everywhere, even among the "ruling classes," and the provision of role models for young gay people. If someone is reluctant or refuses to reveal his or her sexual orientation, Signorile has the remedy—either blatant and dramatic stories, as in the Forbes case, or the innuendo that for some time appeared in his column entitled "Peek A Boo."

Signorile's targets are the famous, the rich, the powerful—in short, the well-known figures of our society. He argues that to be in the closet betrays rank-and-file gay people who have been fighting for years for rights. Most gay activists disagree; they simply see another betrayal. They believe that what Signorile and other "outing" advocates do is to betray years and years of fighting for privacy rights. Clearly, privacy rights are not at the top of Signorile's list of priorities. In fact, he has claimed, in his column in *Outweek*, as well as in the popular press, that the primary concern about privacy for homosexuals belongs to another time.

Tom Stoddard, the thoughtful and dedicated director of the Lambda Defense and Education Fund, believes Signorile's actions are dangerous, reckless, and potentially very harmful to the entire gay community. On the other hand, Larry Kramer, the playwright and committed activist, has called Signorile a modern hero for the gay movement. On balance, however, it appears that even those who disdain those who live secret homosexual lives are troubled by what Michelangelo Signorile has wrought. Civil liberties lawyer Nan Hunter has said that, far from removing a stigma, it increases stigmatization by playing "into the mind-set that homosexuality is a dirty little secret."

Signorile's actions in some ways dismantle one of privacy's paradoxes, while simultaneously creating new ones. To say openly that homosexuality should be recognized and announced and that attempts should stop being made to hide under the protective cover of constitutional privacy does reduce the contradiction of gay pride.

On the other hand, for a gay activist to reveal the private sexual behavior of others, against their will, is to render a large part of the struggle for gay rights even more paradoxical. The court cases about homosexual rights have traditionally been fought around the issue that to invade another's bedroom ought to be so disgusting to all Americans that it should be forbidden. What Signorile has done is open the door to the bedrooms of his own brothers and sisters. In the words of one activist, Stuart Kellogg, former editor of the *Advocate*, "If we don't want policemen coming into our bedrooms, we have to safeguard other people's privacy too."

Signorile and his colleagues are not a part of the sexual privacy conversation. Theirs is, instead, the conversation of the rights of minorities. He makes the argument repeatedly that to be homosexual is the same issue as being black, or a member of any other minority, and that just as it is unthinkable that one would deny one's own race, so it is equally unthinkable that homosexuals should be afforded the right to keep their sexual life a secret. This is rather simplistic thinking, for it is surely not the case that all members of all races or religious groups always identify with their own group. Both literature and social research are filled with stories of people who chose to be identified with something else.

The question of the proper status for homosexuality is, of course, not the salient issue here. It is instead the question of what an ideal world might look like with regard to sexual choice. Signorile's actions suggest that in a perfect world, devoid of intolerance, *all* homosexuals would want to be known as such, and would so proclaim themselves voluntarily and in a public fashion. Is it not also possible that, in a world free of hatred and prejudice, some few homosexuals would feel that they had finally earned the right to complete privacy and to lives without the fear of revelation and its attendant costs and punishments? Whatever the case, the fight for complete protection for homosexuals is centered around the belief that all private actions must be in the complete control of the individuals involved.

To be pushed unwillingly out of the closet and into a society that still has so far to go with regard to its feelings about sexuality is at best hurtful, and at worst, tragic. Whether or not at the hands of a gay activist, this kind of invasion is a tool aimed at making an already vulnerable minority all the more frightened and vulnerable. Pushing people out, against their wishes, is a highly questionable device for making more friends for the gay rights movement. The irrefutable issue is that all people, even famous ones, ought to have the right to their own revelation policies with regard to their sexuality.

Signorile, and the staff at *Outweek*, believe that the refusal of the press to reveal the homosexual identities of closeted people is a further indication of just how homophobic the American press is. Perhaps?

Perhaps it is also the case that some journalists and others believe that the people who have to live in a society where they have yet to be protected by a full blanket of liberties and rights ought to be able to decide the degree of their own vulnerability and ought to be permitted to manage their own risk-taking.

Legitimacy and Recognition:
A Stake in the System

> I can only hope that the Court soon will re-
> consider its analysis and conclude that depriving
> individuals of the right to choose for themselves
> how to conduct their intimate relationships poses
> a far greater threat to the values most deeply
> rooted in our nation's history than tolerance of
> non-conformity could ever do. Because I think
> the Court today betrays those values, I dissent.
> *Justice Harry Blackmun, from his dissent in* Hard-
> wick

We have not afforded homosexuals the privacy of the bedroom, nor has our "voyeurism" granted them the dignity of the deathbed. Homosexuals have successfully announced their sexuality and their sorrow, but they have not found a way to convince us that their kind of family is perhaps the most illustrative of the "new family" to which so much media attention has been devoted.

Just as the word *survival* implies a struggle to remain alive, not necessarily the savoring of existence during the battle to preserve one's status of "among the living," so AIDS has replaced the celebratory element of gay pride. Illness, even AIDS, must not and cannot define human rights, nor should it set its parameters.

To fight the good fight for equal rights and fair treatment using only AIDS as the backdrop does a disservice to the life that most homosexuals will be fortunate (or condemned) to go on living. Earlier I suggested that long after we had found a cure for AIDS we would still be confronted with our dismal failure as a society to find a code of civilized ethics for privacy under siege. The opposite of this seems to be true as it applies to the victimized. That is, when the gay community is no longer attacked by AIDS, they will be faced with the dire inadequacy of their protections as *living* citizens. One needs to be entitled to fairness in housing, jobs, access to the rights that accompany marriage, equality in health and retirement benefits, and the panoply of other liberties and entitlements when one is a healthy homosexual as well as a sick one.

> Even otherwise deeply closeted gay men and lesbians are avid in their testimonials about the need to wage war against the disease. But too many of these AIDS crusaders never go public over the right of homosexuals to something more than not dying.... A certain interest in AIDS has become the trendy code for suggesting one's homosexuality without declaring it, what being a bachelor and an artiste used to suggest.
> *Darrel Yates Rist, "The Deadly Costs of an Obsession,"* The Nation *(February 13, 1989)*

Rist makes the point that the concentration on death as an obsession is costly to the gay community because it presents gays as victims of disease, not of oppression and intolerance.

This concentration on the tragedy of AIDS masks the gay community's vulnerability as much as it highlights it. Rist goes on to a more exact point:

> The ruse that comforts us is that the fight against AIDS and the struggle for gay rights are the same. . . . For, though the constituencies of gay rights and AIDS activism may overlap, the politics—as conceived—are often violently incompatible. At the October 1987 National March on Washington for Lesbian and Gay Rights, an uncommon show of militant self-respect among homosexuals, at least a half-million of us paraded not just against AIDS but for all the rights and privileges that heterosexuals enjoy. Yet, even as we rallied, I sat in a meeting of national AIDS activists who fretted over the possibility that the event would become a political embarrassment for AIDS lobbyists. The symbolic public same-sex wedding the Saturday before the march, a demonstration for spousal rights, was a particular sore point. The director of a powerful national AIDS umbrella organization especially complained that when the wedding hit the news a disgusted Congress would renege on AIDS funding. . . .

AIDS, as it has affected the gay community, is after all the disease of love, or at least of the fling. Whether the encounter that caused the disease in the victim was the result of a romantic attachment is not, for the moment, the issue. AIDS has become a romanticized event, in an underromanticized community.

If you doubt this to be correct, imagine a poignant, compelling film, play, or art exhibit dedicated to the subject of AIDS and the junkie community. AIDS as the result of an encounter with a dirty needle is not the "normal heart" to which the activist and playwright Larry Kramer referred in his play of the same name.

What does an AIDS mentality for homosexuals suggest? It takes us back to the sort of preoccupations that horrified Susan Sontag with regard to cancer and, before that, tuberculosis. The romanticization of dread illness, even if it be in the name of protest, outrage, or courage, nonetheless diminishes the human being who is something beyond his or her illness, something more than a person fighting to stay alive against a dread killer. Chronic and fatal illness, however valiantly the person wages the war, is to some extent the reverse of life. It is the preoccupation with the reality and notion of death or the prayer for its absence or its delay; it is not the validation of life.

What we as a society do when we say that a group cannot be recognized legally because it is so nonconforming, or dangerous, or offensive, is to force confrontation of a public nature. The gays forced into the streets proclaiming their sexuality is the metaphor for this confrontation. We have stipulated that they do not belong, that their intimate acts done even in complete privacy are illegal, and that their public existence in some major way is therefore illegitimate. We are saying: you cannot obtain a recognized status because your private acts are invalid and your public displays obnoxious or embarrassing—never apparently extrapolating that the two are inextricably linked and that the invalidation of the private life may have led to the public crying out and then to complicating and sometimes destructive behaviors in a health crisis. We need to recognize that commonplace of political and civic life: the responsible and involved person/citizen is the one who feels she or he has a real stake in the system. To deny homosexuals a rightful, recognized, and legitimate place in the American system (writ large) harms the entire body politic.

Recognized rituals legitimate our actions, define and lend meaning to our relationships, and shape cultural norms. Family rituals: a birthday, a wedding anniversary, the date a family member died, Christmas, Chanukah, the first snowfall, the Fourth of July—special meals, a favorite restaurant, a park, a picnic, a walk, a sleigh ride, candles kindled, prayers recited. Rituals accompany our celebrations and our sorrows.

Families, especially, assign meanings to events. These are private, sometimes serious, sometimes frivolous and endearing rituals. They are the things families do in code, as a way of saying to each other: we are a family; we have continuity, meaning, significance. The fact that certain rituals accompany certain holidays or family anniversary dates has been the stuff of much literature and not a few family squabbles when a ritual is mistakenly forgotten or altered. The British anthropologist Mary Douglas has written of the significance of food in ritual, and indeed the preparation of certain foods often accompanies a family's celebrations.

These are intimate rituals, and they differ from family to family, but they can be observed as attentively and systematically as if they were part of a rigidly proscribed cultural or religious order. Family rituals are self-defined and exist by the mutual consent (or at least, the indulgence) of the individual members of a collective, which we have come to label the "family." Perhaps private family rituals now stem, as extensions, from the public rituals that mark certain life events and calendar celebrations. Historians tell us that originally it worked the other way around—the private family rituals accompanying marriage, birth, and death eventually became incorporated into the external and public structure of nation and church.

A Christian baptism is different from a Jewish baby naming or briss. And still different is an American Indian custom of naming a baby by first whispering the name into the infant's ear so that the baby is the first person ever to hear its name spoken and then the baby, by name, is presented to the assembled tribe. Jewish weddings differ from Catholic weddings, from Muslim weddings, and so on. These public rituals have something in common, however—they signify membership.

The public rituals of family life are the very manifestation of its centrality and importance in our culture. The family, writ large, is seen as the accepted and recognized unit of society. Families give meaning and texture to the fabric of our customs and our laws. It is the commonly understood legitimacy of the family that makes it such a powerful fortress of protection and of recognition. The definition of what constitutes a family has moved from the extended family of the last century to the nuclear family of the 1940s and 1950s.

Today the notion of family is in upheaval. Abundant divorces have created layered or sandwiched families that include stepchildren and stepparents and stepgrand-parents incorporating multiple family units. These merged and reconstituted families have their own private rituals as well as receiving the customary nod of approval or recognition as a family. Scores of households are headed by single parents, and these too fall within our definition of the family.

The family unit still in search of validation and its ac-companying dignity is the homosexual couple. For homo-sexuals, then, these rituals have remained private, if not secretive. Homosexual ritual is primarily a way of com-municating in code. Even couples of the same sex who have lived together for a very long time are unlikely to receive a ready nod of societal approval. Despite isolated cases that have ruled a family status for apartment leases, insurance benefits, and the like, homosexual couples still fight for any uniform protection. Lesbians still find them-selves in courtrooms defending their rights as mothers and fighting to maintain custody of their own children. While obviously not precluded from having their own private rituals, the unrecognized and unapproved fact of a homosexual family status excludes gay people from the official rituals of affirmation.

Homosexuals can be denied even the basic and customary rights and usual entitlements of a relationship. A case involving a lesbian couple has become a particularly painful and bitter symbol to the homosexual community. A woman named Sharon Kowalski was injured in an accident some years ago. Her parents successfully kept Kowalski's lover, Karen Thompson, from having any contact with her. The case was in and out of a series of lower courts. Eventually the women did prevail. However, the case clearly points out that without a family or spousal status, there is little likelihood of normal relationship rights, even intimate ones, without battle and struggle. (In August 1989, New York City took one small hopeful step with regard to its city workers by stipulating through Executive Order 123 that the principle of domestic partnerships had to be recognized.)

Whether inside the protected enclave of family grouping or in the external world of religious and national custom and tradition, ritual is recognition. But it is only the religious, civil, or legal ritual that legitimates actions and provides certain guarantees by stamping "acceptable" on the participants. Private rituals without any corresponding public acknowledgment remain within the purview of intimate and tender shared moments and as such have no currency in the world of reality.

There have, of course, been public homosexual rituals. These rituals, however, have not centered on individual relationships or on the validity of their existence as an authentic, if unique, family unit. The earliest rituals marked homosexuality qua homosexuality—that is, in the display of the sexual component of one's life at the loss of the personal; the exposure of one's sexuality at the cost of one's heart, perhaps. These rituals began with the emerging, somewhat sporadic gay parades, which have finally become the regular and annual gay pride day commemorations.

The gay male community has put much ritual into the sorry business of dying. The Names Project is an enormous patchwork quilt, each square commemorating the life and death of an AIDS victim. On Friday, December 1, 1989, many museums and galleries across the country observed a "no art" day when exhibits were closed, paintings taken down or draped, to remind people symbolically of the loss AIDS has wrought. These are the rituals of struggle, of sorrow, of tragedy, not of validation, legitimacy, and celebration.

These are the stories of homosexual lives, or the stories of their dying. Whether they are stories of lives or deaths, the reality of gay life makes us ask: "Who should define what constitutes a family?" What do we do to homosexuals when we say "You are not, and cannot be, a family"? Even if you have lived in the same home with the same person for twenty-five years, raised children, pooled your resources, built your dreams together, triumphed and failed together, your intimate moments are valid only as secret acts; they have no link to the world of legal guarantees and protections. There is no sanction for your existence as a family nor, ironically, any real security for your private acts. We do not need the same kind of permission to exist inside the family—to justify our existence—as we do outside in the larger society. However carefully the details are attended to or how faithfully or routinely observed, private rituals are not vehicles toward a status of legitimacy.

Until there is recognition of this family unit, their rituals are hollow and they are effectively robbed of a strategy for recognition and protection. Perhaps the preoccupation with AIDS that has captured the gay community and, to some extent, the elements of the sympathetic straight community has another, darker, more sinister side. That is simply that our willing or available validation of homosexuality seems to be in our recognition of its passing numbers due to a tragic, cataclysmic disease.

Part Four

Last Rights

Privacy and Death

*Going to a Place Called
"To Die"*

Ten years ago one of my closest friends died. She was thirty-five years old and left behind three small children, aged four, five, and six and a stunned, grieving husband. We buried her on her youngest son's fourth birthday. The details of Susan's last year of life made the movie *Terms of Endearment*, an almost shameless tearjerker, seem like pretty weak stuff.

The quest to find the final, fateful diagnosis was a relentless year of doctors, tests, and finally, cerebral probings better reserved for a science fiction novel than for the skull of one of your dearest friends. Every diagnostic and medical analytic tool was employed in the hope that what was wrong with Susan was anything but something serious or terminal.

In the early days the complaints were minimal. A slight numbness in one hand, more pronounced when she tried to play the stringed instruments she loved, including her piano; slightly blurred vision; a loss of equilibrium from time to time. I wanted it to be simple, an inner ear problem, perhaps. The first doctor wanted it to be psychological—too much stress, too many children too close together. Or "boredom," as another suggested, simple "housewife syndrome," he stated. She was a gifted mathematician, teacher, artist, musician. For him the answer was undoubtedly that she was bored because her duties were, at that moment, more centered on mothering.

Those were not the answers, and as much as I raved at the "piggish" qualities of that doctor and his antiwoman sentiments, somehow I prayed that he was right and that Susan was wrong. She had suspected all too soon that the problem was a big one.

Susan announced the end when the symptoms were far too minor to do so, yet she sensed from the earliest moments that something had gone very awry. None of us wanted to hear it. We cajoled; we were tough—we told her to get a grip on herself and to stop being dramatic— she wasn't going to die.

From the beginning she felt the presence of an unwelcome and unfriendly intruder. All too soon the symptoms became too numerous to ignore—eggs cracked on the floor because the bowl was somehow missed; serious stumbling trying in vain to find a low step on a path, followed then by terrible falls on the street; stabbing at her food trying to locate it on her plate. After more than six months of probings, just after Thanksgiving, after yet another horrific surgical procedure aimed at fixing what was supposed to be only a passing problem, we finally learned what was really wrong.

The doctors had belatedly discovered what Susan had always sensed: a brain tumor.

Malignant? Probably not.

Inoperable? Definitely.

Fatal? Positively.

I remember everything about that hospital room the night I went to see her after the diagnosis. Every detail is registered in my mind in a strange kind of grim and blurry precision. I remember the color of the walls—a sickening and overpowering green, which in a gruesome symmetry coordinated all too perfectly with the surgical greens of the roving medical staff.

Mostly, I remember every word she said that night. She told me with great rage about the way the doctors had told her their diagnosis, apparently treating her like a small child or someone unable to comprehend the simplest language. At the end they asked her, "Do you understand what we have told you?" "Yes," she said. "You have told me that I am going to die, and that I am going to die quickly."

She recounted, with considerable pride and strength, that at that point she turned away from them and looked out the window at what she could see of San Francisco. Her business with the medical profession was finished.

That night Susan told me, as she had told her husband and other family members, that she immediately wanted two things. She wanted to go home to be with her children those last remaining weeks, and to die, and she wanted to go out to her favorite Chinese restaurant for dinner.

We all managed to grant Susan that first wish. She was too sick and too frail far too quickly for any of us to contemplate her second wish. What ensued for the next months is a chronicle of dying—twenty-four-hour nursing care, an almost constant vigil among family and her closest friends, a flurry of temporary hope that maybe the progress of the tumor would not be so fast, followed by unrelieved sorrow and grief, and an incredible and blinding rage at life's capricious and unfair turns. And finally, the prayer and wish that each day might be her last—the hope for the end.

Once Susan had lost consciousness completely and we could no longer make any real contact with her, I used to think, while sitting next to her bed, or downstairs in the rooms she loved, that she was in a tunnel—that death was ultimately a journey through a tunnel. Once in, you cannot back out, and once in, before you arrive at the end of the tunnel, the suffering can be so severe that you cannot imagine there is light at the end. Watching her slip away, seeing how difficult it was, how much pain there was, I wondered if she feared she would never emerge. I wondered if she could still think, and if she could, did she think that it would never be over, that she would never move into another reality. Whatever that is—that nonliving, nonearthly, other reality.

148

During this time of waiting, of counting days, Susan's youngest son asked me an unforgettable question. In a terribly mature voice he said, "Is mommy going to die?" The family policy, from the beginning, was to tell the complete truth, whatever the question from the children. I turned to face him directly and said quietly but clearly, "Yes, she is going to die."

He seemed quite unshaken by it and then said, "When she goes to Die, can we take an airplane to go visit her?" "To Die" was a place, like taking an airplane to New York to visit his grandparents. Those tragic little words come back to me often as I observe how too many of us die and how little we want to plan for that last trip.

Despite all of the desperate sorrow over the termination of Susan's life at thirty-five, and the drama, and the relentless pain of the last months, her death was a private matter. She had done the negotiation. There would be no intrusion from strangers filing lawsuits on her behalf. There would be no medical heroics. When she finally left us that February, her departure was unaided by technology. She was assisted through the ordeal only by pain medication and the minimal humane procedures. At the end she was surrounded only by her family, her dearest friends, and a private nurse. She died in her own home.

Although it occurred in the post–Karen Ann Quinlan age of technological death, with its attendant moral and ethical problems, Susan's death was an old-fashioned kind of death. She died the way we used to die, privately, and usually in our own homes. Before the supposed

149

miracles of modern medicine, death resulting from incurable illness or a terrible accident had a more predictable pattern. There was a ritual of dying; death, known and recognized as unavoidable, was perhaps less feared. In any event, it was certainly less denied than in our own age.

Freedom to Die

Whether we began life in the traditional way, our births "shrouded in mystery," or first as a laboratory frozen zygote, later implanted in the womb of a woman who would not be the mother who raised us, we all will come, eventually, to the same end. Unfortunately, however, we do not all reach this last stop in the same way. We hope for ourselves and for our family and friends that we will have an easy death.

And some of us will have very easy deaths, at an appropriate elderly age. Others of us will have beleaguered, prolonged, unspeakably painful deaths. Yet another segment of us will have tragic, but quick, deaths due to a variety of nightmarish accidents. More tragically, some of us will hang in a suspended form of life known as a "persistent vegetative state." While few of us look forward to the time when we are finished with our lives, our desire not to have a terrible time over the chore of dying is universal.

How to die? Or how will we be allowed to die? These questions have become part of the dialogue around this most vexing public policy dilemma.

Raging against death lost its romantic nineteenth-century appeal with the advent of medical heroics against death, or at least, against the cessation of breathing. Has technologically advanced medicine given us the option of an easier death? Or has it primarily raised the spectre of a feared dread existence sustained at half-life, or far, far less? In our age, our goal might very well be to strive for an easy, quick death.

While death will not be the height of our life's experience and hardly a joyous passage, our departure ought to be as free of as much pain as possible. And certainly our pending death should not be wrought with public legal battles and court fights with complete strangers. We must come to a policy for "last rights" that can protect the individual, the family, the medical practitioners, and, of course, the state's presumed benign interest in preserving life.

If one is sure that his or her own death is approaching or that the pain or disability from an illness is too much to endure, and is still fortunate to be lucid and somewhat mobile, then the question can be: how to die with dignity and with grace?

In 1983 Elizabeth Bouvia said she was ready to die, and she hoped to do so with both dignity and grace. A victim of cerebral palsy, the then young woman in her late twenties, was confined to a wheelchair. The only independent movement of her body was her ability to move a hand, ever so slightly. She was married for a time, was able to conceive a child but miscarried, and did graduate from

151

college. Yet she had no sustaining relationship, no family ties, and no possibility of employment.

She was in excruciating pain most of the time from arthritis. Life held little appeal for Elizabeth Bouvia. Journalists and medical professionals at the time cited her difficult nature and her barely concealed rage—a legitimate rage, for surely Ms. Bouvia was entitled to rail against the fates that had dealt her such a hand in life. Elizabeth Bouvia not only was ready to die but had a plan. She intended to stop eating and to have the hospital where she was a patient take care of her pain needs until she died. She demanded that they assist her and that they provide her no nutrition. The superior court for the state of California said that Bouvia had no right to insist that a hospital perform an illegal act. Her request, according to the judge, was to ask a hospital to act as an assistant to a crime—the crime of suicide. Bouvia insisted that she should not have her right to end her life taken from her just because she was incapable of acting on her desires.

What followed was a byzantine series of maneuvers to find the freedom to die—ending in Tijuana, where she tried to starve herself to death in a motel room. Starving to death may be a private business when done in a motel room in a foreign country, but it is not a pleasant or an easy task. After a few days she backed out of her plan and had her hopes raised by a kind friend who convinced her, temporarily, to work on getting better.

There could be no miracle cures for Elizabeth Bouvia's

ravaged and broken body. Eventually she ended up in another California hospital, this time force-fed. She did not give up her legal struggle, and finally the appeals court of California said that the decision to end her life was hers and that a hospital was not entitled to continue to force-feed her against her will.

The lower court's decision had really said that a community was not obligated to help a person commit suicide and could not be forced to participate. The implication of the reversal by the California state court of appeals is that suicide is such a private and morally individual act that it must reside in the person alone. Both decisions are rooted in a rational approach to life and death, and although in disagreement with each other, they share an irrefutable logic and stem from our conflicting traditions of individual liberty versus the responsibilities of the public weal.

Like Elizabeth Bouvia, Larry James McAfee depends on others for the physical acts that keep him alive. As a quadriplegic, completely paralyzed from an accident, he quite successfully uses a mouth-controlled device to move his wheelchair. The respirator that keeps him alive sits in the bottom of the wheelchair and is not controlled by him. For the past few years, Larry James McAfee has been reviewing his life and trying to decide whether to live or to die. His is not the poetic review of death, the territory of the dark poets; his is not the "special language of suicide" that filled Anne Sexton's verses.

Until very recently, Mr. McAfee's battle was a legal one, fought with the state, to be allowed to control his respirator with his tongue, so he could take his life if and when he chose. The state of Georgia had initially seen this as legalizing suicide or murder, but has finally granted him that right.

He is not a romantic figure, but he certainly is a public one. What he decides in the coming months (and he is not at all certain now that he wants to die) will be reported in detail on the front pages of the tabloids and the venerated mainline newspapers and news magazines of the land. There he is for us to view, a quadriplegic, with tubes coming out of his mouth, incapacitated from an accident, his psychological temperature reported in grimacing minute detail.

Mr. McAfee's soul has been splayed for us to see its inner workings. And, if Mr. McAfee decides, that he is so suffused with the pain and emptiness of his life, that he wants to die, his death will not have the romantic overtones of Sylvia Plath's foreshortened life amidst the bread crumbs of her oven.

He is a symbol, as several before him, of the right to control one's death choices. Mr. McAfee also represents our incapacity to value the disabled. But, perhaps most of all, Larry James McAfee lies before us totally exposed. Apparently, we have come to believe that to expose more and more details about the ill, the paralyzed, and the dying is an acceptable national custom.

From Quinlan to Cruzan—
Worse Than Death

When a person ceases to be anything but a breathing body, families desiring control assert that the person in question certainly would not want to exist that way. Even without substantial documentation that this was the person's wish, and absent sworn statements witnessing that the person was heard to say such a thing, it is hard to imagine anyone who would knowingly choose to go on in that way. While one can hypothesize that some people might prefer life, even at this substrata, to facing death, it is, in any event, unlikely to be a large group of us.

It is here inside the realm of the family, however, that we find another of privacy's many contradictions. In the abortion battle, pro-choice advocates argue strongly that a minor child should have the right to choose to have an abortion, without either the consent, or the knowledge, of her parents.

Privacy, in this case, is seen as appropriately resting within the young woman, and not within the family. To require a young woman to reveal her pregnancy in order to activate the guarantee of *Roe* in some real sense invalidates the privacy basis of that abortion decision. Yet, in the right-to-die cases, we find exactly the opposite privacy claim. The advocates of the right to die argue that the family must be seen as the repository of individual

privacy, that the legitimate claim to privacy for a comatose patient transfers from the individual to the family
involved.

> Death is sometimes not the worst situation you
> can be in.
> *Nancy Cruzan, as reported by her sister, in the Sup-
> reme Court brief filed for the family*

To be able to look at questions surrounding these
rights, we need to separate the dying from the comatose.
And those who are comatose, brain dead, or damaged
beyond repair must be separated from those in comas,
where there is at least a chance of recovery, or even partial
recovery. Perhaps the most troubling legal battles have
centered around a family's right to control the treatment
of a comatose family member.

In reality, these cases are more about the *timing* of
death than about the occurrence of death. That is, when
the irreversibility of the situation is clear, the question
becomes whether to sustain them in such a condition,
where their faculties are so considerably diminished or,
in some cases, absent, or whether to decide to quicken
their demise by withdrawing life-support machinery.

We fill our language surrounding death with euphemisms—a "living will" for a document that instructs people how we want, not to live, but to die; "passing away,"
instead of dying, or "she didn't make it" rather than "she
died on the operating table," and so forth. In some circumstances, the phrase "right to die" is also a bit of a eu-

phemism. When a person is hopelessly and seemingly eternally unconscious, we are also talking about the rights of other people, or another person, to make a decision.

The right to die, in the comatose patient, is the delegation of a right, a question of who should or can morally or legally, say: *Now* is the time for this death to occur, not later. When a person can no longer make that choice for him- or herself, it is an awesome and frightening responsibility for another to take. In this domain, privacy loses its status as an individual right and moves to reside instead within a family.

In the cases when a family has asked to be given the right to end life-sustaining treatment, something else, something besides the patient's presumed wishes, is also operative—the right of the family itself to determine the quality of its communal life. To be honest, we are also talking about the wishes of the family, not just the patient.

Does a family have the right to say that they cannot (that they choose not) to sustain endlessly a family member in a vegetative state? Over and above "the wishes of the patient," does a family have that right, to say that they are both financially and emotionally exhausted and that they must end the situation? And while the state has a compelling interest in "preserving life," does the state not also have a compelling moral obligation to define *life* in a way that precludes the state from spending its precious resources on the constant medical care of thousands of citizens who are "dead, but living"?

During 1975 and 1976 an event in New Jersey first focused our national attention on how *not* to die. The name Karen Ann Quinlan became synonymous with the fight for the right to die. All over the country, family members were saying to each other versions of "Don't let me end up a Quinlan." Survey researchers incorporated her name into question items in opinion polls about privacy in death, the right to die, and euthanasia. The "Quinlan standard" has been applied in a number of other cases where a court of law and judges have been asked to make a decision about who can discontinue a life-support mechanism for a comatose patient.

The Quinlan case was prominent in the press for more than two years, but, it never went beyond the legal system in the state of New Jersey. It would take another decade and a half for a right-to-die case to be heard by the Supreme Court of the United States (the Nancy Cruzan case originating in Missouri).

No one is really sure how Karen Quinlan became hopelessly comatose. She had been drifting a bit, apparently, as young people sometimes do. She had started to drink and to engage in that often lethal practice of combining drinking with "popping" pills. Whatever was happening on the night of April 14, 1975, Karen Ann, twenty-one years of age, stopped functioning in any humanly recognizable way. Her parents held out hope; they continued a bedside vigil and tried all possible medical treatments for more than five months. Finally, strengthened by the comfort offered from their friends and with the spiritual aid of their family priest, they asked the doctors to remove the respirator from Karen Ann. The doctors refused.

Julia and Joseph Quinlan, who had adopted Karen Ann when she was an infant, asked the court for relief. In the pleading filed with the court, their lawyer, Paul Armstrong, asked that the Quinlan daughter be "allowed to die with grace and dignity."

The lower court judge for the state of New Jersey said no. To do so, against the doctors' desires, was to interfere with proper medical jurisdiction, and the removal of a respirator might include a charge of homicide as well.

The Quinlans appealed to New Jersey's highest court, the state supreme court, who found for the Quinlans. Basing its decision on the state of New Jersey's constitutional provision for privacy, the court said, "Ultimately, there comes a point at which the individual's rights overcome the state's interest."

In a dramatic, media-laden moment, Mr. Quinlan disconnected the respirator attached to his brain-dead comatose daughter. But Karen Ann Quinlan lived on, or breathed on. In a tragically ironic twist, despite medical predictions to the contrary, she stayed in that hopeless state for ten years more before dying in 1985.

At no time during the Quinlans' legal battle, or during the years afterward, did they ever request that the feeding tube be removed. The Quinlans always maintained that they believed that the respirator was causing her discomfort and pain, and that had been their fundamental reason for requesting its removal. They said in interviews at the time, and again when she died in 1985, that they felt that to remove the respirator put Karen Ann in "God's hands," but to remove the feeding tube would be going too far. Her father said: "To remove the feeding tube, that's like saying, 'I'm going to take charge.' ... We know what will happen if we remove it."

Life or Liberty?

> The protection of the Constitution has long been extended to persons unable to speak for themselves. Constitutional liberty and privacy interests of bodily integrity are not cancelled when a citizen falls unconscious or incompetent and thus cannot directly exercise those rights.
> *Brief for the Cruzan family, Supreme Court*

> The state's interest in prolonging life is particularly valid in Nancy's case. Nancy is not terminally ill. Her death is imminent only if she is denied food and water. Medical evidence shows Nancy will continue a life of relatively normal duration if allowed basic sustenance. The state's concern with the sanctity of life rests on the principle that life is precious and worthy of preservation without regard to its quality.
> *Opinion for the Circuit Court of the State of Missouri in* Cruzan

In Missouri, Nancy Cruzan, lies motionless, as she has for more than seven years, speechless, unconscious, and brain damaged. Above her head rages a battle that pits two of America's most honored values against one another: the absolute value of the sanctity of life versus the cherished belief in individual liberty as the preceding quotes illustrate. Nancy Cruzan cannot hear these seemingly irreconcilable voices plead for her fate. She is the latest in a series of cases centering on the rights of a family to control the treatment of a comatose family member. She is, however, the first such case to reach the U.S. Supreme Court.

The *Cruzan* case is a metaphor of "separate conversations." Those who support the family claim that a basic and fundamental liberty is at stake—the right to be free of government intervention in the private value decisions of families. Those who argue against the family, in actuality, rarely make a specific reference to the condition of Nancy Cruzan—for them it is the absolute and abstract notion of life that is at issue. Life itself is valid and must be sustained regardless of the circumstances.

This is the same division that occurs in the abortion battle—the ultimate value of human life in a deadly conflict with the right of control and autonomy. As in the struggle for reproductive choice, two such strong values collide with one another that each side bypasses the critical issue of the other. It is a conflict of value hierarchies and core belief systems where, not surprisingly, resolution and compromise are seemingly impossible.

In the sad land of near-death there are distinctions that are terribly significant. A note on a patient's chart that says "DNR" means Do Not Resuscitate. This is often employed in cases involving either terminally ill patients or the very elderly, who are likely to go into cardiac or respiratory failure. A "DNR" sign is essentially a command to the medical profession that the patient has requested a "natural death."

For the layperson, the term "life support" basically means two things: respirators that keep a person breathing, even when there is total brain damage, and various kinds of feeding tubes that provide calories to the comatose or dying person to keep him or her from starving.

During the Quinlan case the question of removing feeding tubes had not emerged as a national issue with regard to the dying. Since that time, in the state of New Jersey, for example, a supreme court decision in January, 1985 widened a family's control to include the withdrawal of all life-sustaining mechanisms, including any feeding devices, provided that substantial proof could be shown that the patient would have requested this if he or she had been able to request that action.

What the Quinlan case said, and what the family of Nancy Cruzan has alleged before the U.S. Supreme Court in the closing session of 1989, is that they are entitled, *as a family*, to act in the stead of the comatose person, in that person's best interests, and that the state must not interfere. It is a graphic representation of the Brandeis coda—"the right to be let alone."

In June of 1990 the Supreme Court decided that the state of Missouri could sustain the life of Nancy Cruzan, despite her condition. The decision was largely based on the belief of the Court that the Cruzan family had not presented sufficient evidence that Nancy herself would have wanted to terminate medical treatment. Thus, the Cruzan family lost their battle at the highest court of this land.

Of far-reaching note, however, is that the Supreme Court, in its first right-to-die case, supported the notion that there is a constitutional right to reject medical treatment. Every justice, except Justice Scalia, stood behind the opinion that those who have previously expressed, or are presently able to express, their desires clearly regarding their medical treatment have that option as a part of every American's right to liberty under the Constitution.

Guarding Against Guardians:
The Loss of a Safeguard

Both our historic and our legal tradition supports the notion that families should dictate life and death decisions. Most of us are lucky enough to believe that our loved ones would not pull the plug if there was still justifiable hope.

But not all families are totally trustworthy. I know a man who has a "living will" for the express purpose of ensuring that his children cannot, and must not, be asked to make that decision for him. In his case, as in others, a family so governed by greed or anger may not have the best interests of a person in mind if the death of that person would vastly increase the wealth of the surviving children. In other words, there are evil families, greedy families, and disturbed families. Not all of us are safe in life, or near death, with the decisions our families might make for us.

One of the sorrows coming out of the warfare of the abortion controversy is that we have lost an important and valuable safeguard for people in such vulnerable family situations. The concepts of both legal guardianship and the state's interest in preserving life are rooted in the notion of a protective government. This is, in and of itself, not such a bad goal for a decent or humane society. The guardian role has now been usurped by the right-to-life forces, and it is no longer a protective safeguard for the vulnerable. Instead, guardianship in many cases has become a political tool of intrusion.

Because of the distortions wrought by religious ideology, however, these are now the tools of those who are not terribly interested in the legitimate protection of potentially vulnerable citizens. The confusion of religion with politics has turned these public safeguards into devices of despair and destruction for many families. That is, the involvement of the ideological activists has injured these potentially helpful outside protective devices, in some cases rendering them meaningless and, in the worst case, harming the families they were devised to protect.

Increasingly, in cases involving the principle of the right to die (as in the abortion battle), people absolutely unrelated to families believe they are entitled to make the decision for the comatose, or completely impaired, patient. Here again the right-to-life forces (in fact, some of the same people) engage in tactics very similar to those used in the Klein case. Getting themselves appointed as guardians of the patient, they argue on the side of preserving "life," at any level and at any cost.

Mr. Washburn and Baby Jane Doe:
The Greater Tragedy

One of the most flagrant violations of the use of guardianship against a family's rights occurred in New York in the case known as Baby Jane Doe. Baby Jane Doe was born in Long Island in 1983 with a number of birth defects resulting from spina bifida, but also including fluid in her brain. In addition, she was born with a tiny, malformed head as well as other deformities. If untreated by surgical procedures, the baby, it was then anticipated, would probably live no longer than two years. If treated aggressively, with surgical procedures, it was expected that the child might live into her twenties, but that she would be paralyzed, unable to care for herself in any manner, and very severely retarded.

The parents were given a range of three medical treatment options: (1) A surgical procedure could be performed on the spinal column, as well as an elaborate surgical procedure on the brain. (2) Another medical treatment option was to forgo surgery but to provide a thorough antibiotic treatment to keep the open wounds and the spinal cord from becoming infected, and to provide adequate nutrition for the baby. (3) Yet another option was to withhold all medical treatment but to feed the infant and keep her as comfortable as possible.

At that time, the parents in this instance chose the middle course of action. However, Mr. Washburn, that professional "guardian ad litem" (who would later, in 1989, file against Mr. Klein and for the fetus of his comatose wife), tried to become the guardian of Baby Jane Doe. His knowledge of the case was minimal, if not nonexistent. No one is sure just how he found out about the case, but as a right-to-life lawyer he saw this, as all of his later cases, as part of his holy crusade to validate the "sanctity of life" and to save the helpless from the vile hands of their family members.

The lower court did appoint him guardian, which therefore would have allowed him to direct that the surgery be performed on Baby Jane Doe. However, the New York State court of appeals was very quick to reverse the finding and to hold that the parents, not Mr. Washburn, had made the best decision for their child.

The appellate court based its ruling on procedural grounds, however, and as such did not confront directly the question of the child's best interests. Instead the court held that the state's statutory laws set out very specific procedures for overturning parental choices in such matters through the agencies of the child welfare services. Therefore, the court had rejected Washburn's bid on the grounds that proper procedures were not followed. Yet the appellate court of New York State did say that to allow anyone to interfere at whim with family privacy and responsibilities, without resort to prescribed family court procedures, would "have far-reaching implications." The court went on to condemn the fact that a family had been dragged so suddenly through the court system in such a private and tragic matter.

If the proper procedures had been followed in the case of Baby Jane Doe, and if, by fate and the political tone of the day, the family court was stocked with a set of right-to-life judges, the outcome would also have had "far-reaching implications." This is precisely why so many advocates for privacy see the appointment of the judiciary, at both the state and the federal levels, as so critical to the maintenance of personal liberty.

In many ways the above is not the full story of Baby Jane Doe; Baby Jane Doe is also the story of the distortion of the "state's interest in preserving life." The Reagan administration pressed into service in this case one of their favored weapons. They asked for a judicial reinterpretation of the Rehabilitation Act of 1973. This Act prohibits discrimination against the handicapped. The Reagan administration launched a full-scale campaign to extend this proscription to the withholding of medical treatment for babies like Baby Jane Doe.

Based on its request for a judicial reinterpretation, the administration then demanded that the hospital involved turn over all its records on Baby Jane Doe to determine whether such discrimination had in fact taken place. This was their attempt to circumvent privacy considerations, for the supposed higher good of eliminating discrimination. The hospital refused; the government sued. It was at this point that the parents of Baby Jane Doe became actively involved in the litigation.

This case was not a singular incident; there were other Baby Doe cases. In fact, President Reagan pressed for "Baby Doe regulations" from his earliest days in office. By 1982 the administration had in place an emergency twenty-four-hour telephone number whereby anyone could (anonymously) report a suspicious treatment of any infant. Any hospital failing to provide food or life-saving surgical or medical treatment to infants like Baby Jane Doe would lose their federal funding. This intrusion was justified by the 1973 Rehabilitation Act forbidding discrimination against the handicapped. This was the precise Act that would be brought into the Baby Jane Doe litigation.

The legal counsel for the hospital and the parents stated that the statute was inapplicable to Baby Jane Doe, that records were protected by federal constitutional privacy rights, and furthermore that such disclosure would violate doctor-patient confidentiality. The court held that the parents and the hospital were right, and that the Rehabilitation Act was indeed inapplicable in this instance. The court said that while Baby Jane Doe could, legitimately, be considered handicapped, within the meaning of the 1973 Act, she was not "subject to discrimination."

Although it wouldn't be until 1989 that the U.S. Supreme Court agreed to hear a right-to-die case (Cruzan), the Court did take up the issue of the family's right to control the medical decisions for babies like Baby Jane Doe in 1986. The Supreme Court took a dim view of the Reagan administration's attempt to gain access to the hospital records in that case, and in general foreclosed the Baby Doe regulations and weakened the forces of the right-to-life squads to some extent by stipulating that these impaired infants were not subject to discrimination as handicapped citizens under the 1973 Rehabilitation Act.

The Court's language was most encouraging for those fighting for individual rights in these cases. The opinion was written by Justice John Paul Stevens, who essentially said that while these infants might indeed be handicapped, nothing in our federal laws suggested that hospitals treat these infants without the informed consent of the parents. Justice Stevens steered far from the moral and ethical dilemmas concerning the ultimate destinies of these infants, but his words with regard to federal intrusion were sharp.

In his opinion he also dealt, indirectly perhaps, with the option of taking these ideological campaigns through the ordinary child social welfare agencies when he said that these agencies and organizations "must not be conscripted against their will in a federal crusade."

For Their Own Good:
Death or Murder?

Whether it is a just born, desperately abnormal infant, an elderly unconscious parent with terminal cancer, or a comatose young son or daughter, brain dead from an accident, these are people who cannot speak for themselves. These are those who, involuntarily, must rely on the judgments of others. Surrounding the question of dying is not simply the line between life and death but also the definition of what constitutes murder. There are incidents where one family member has ended the life an another—presumably out of love and for their own good. Whatever the underlying motivation, these are unmistakably acts of desperation. Tragically, "real murder" does occur in families pushed beyond the limit of endurance and where no relief seems possible.

A California man in a hospital, dying of AIDS and in horrible pain, is shot and killed at point-blank pistol range by his friend, who then turns the gun on himself and commits suicide. A wife in Chicago finds her suffering from multiple sclerosis over because her husband shoots her in the head on Christmas night. A Florida man kills his wife, suffering from Alzheimer's disease, because he says they "had a pact" never to let the other one deteriorate into such a condition.

These are the products of good intentions, "mercy killings," perhaps, but not tender or gentle or quiet deaths. Are these not acts of violence but instead intimate acts within a family's right to privacy? While I would argue that these people ought not to be prosecuted for their actions, neither can we condone this as a standard or routine part of the privacy guarantees.

Less violent, but no less desperate, acts surround dying. A Chicago father holds a gun on a hospital staff with one hand and with the other disconnects a life-support system from his tiny child and cradles him as he dies in his arms. Three adult children in Brooklyn, New

York, keep physicians at bay and disconnect the respirator keeping their elderly father alive.

There are a myriad of complications that might have contributed to the above desperate acts requiring individuals to act on their own, without professional help or against medical help—for example, the malpractice possibilities, the conflict of interest between state and individual when the state foots the bill for long-term care, the particular doctor or hospital's religious affiliation, and so forth.

There are, each day, occurrences of euthanasia that are kinder, less hysterical, and more appropriate to an already suffering patient. Increasingly, AIDS victims, in the last painful stages of that devastating disease, are finding help to die. Pills and the potions of death are beginning to be passed on to those desiring them. Yet these are risky acts; to aid in death is still to aid in murder, or to be an accomplice to a suicide. Doctors are understandably concerned about their roles. They can be the victims of prosecution, even when the person receiving a lethal injection or the like is their own family member.

It is too easy, too cheap a line of inquiry, to blame the medical profession, and doctors especially, for the profound mess we are in. Doctors, too, suffer from our cultural ambivalence about how to manage death. The distinguished documentary filmmaker Fred Wiseman produced a grim, but heroic, six-hour look at death, entitled *Near Death*. It illustrated vividly and sympathetically the complicated role of the physician in these decisions.

Doctors must perform the most delicate of balancing acts: allegiance to their profession and to their oath to preserve and sustain life; their commitment and ethical standard toward their patient; their completely human feelings of empathy for the family; their own understandable feelings of frustration, perhaps of personal failure; and the reality of malpractice liability, the larger considerations of law, of state, and national policies.

For some doctors, the directive to turn off the machinery is an impossibility, even when required to do so by a court of law. These are doctors who, because of their personal histories, or spiritual convictions, or a variety of other factors, are simply not able to perform that task as part of their medical duties. Should we require them to do so, despite their objections, whether spiritually, morally, or ethically based? Just as all doctors do not perform abortions, despite a ruling (however weakened) that such procedures are legal, all doctors should not be required to perform the final act of removing life supports.

Richard Selzer has provided one of the best, and most moving, accounts of the tightrope a doctor walks in these critical moments. In his book *Letters to a Young Doctor*, he tells of a wife and a mother eager to see the death of their husband and son because his suffering was so great and so prolonged:

> "I won't let you suffer," I tell him. In his struggle the
> sheet is thrust aside. I see the old abandoned incision,
> the belly stuffed with tumor. His penis, even, is skinny.
> One foot with five blue toes is exposed. In my cupped

172

hand, they are cold. I think of the twenty bones of that foot laced together with tendon, each ray accompanied by its own nerve and artery. Now, this foot seems a beautiful dead animal that had once been trained to transmit the command of a man's brain to earth.

"I'll get rid of the pain," I tell his wife.

But there is no way to kill the pain without killing the man who owns it. Morphine to the lethal dose . . . and still he miaows and bays and makes other sounds like a boat breaking up in a heavy sea. I think his pain will live on long after he dies.

"Please," begs his wife, "we cannot go on like this."

"Do it," says the old woman, his mother. "Do it now."

"To give him any more would kill him," I tell her.

"Then do it," she says.

. . . The women turn to leave. There is neither gratitude nor reproach in their gaze. I should be hooded.

"Listen," I say. "I can get rid of the pain" . . . "with these". . . .

"Yes," he gasps, "yes."

. . . When they are all given, I pull out the needle. A drop of blood blooms on his forearm. I blot it with the alcohol sponge. It is done. In less than a minute, it is done.

. . . The familiar emaciated body untenses. The respirations slow down. Eight per minute . . . six . . . it won't be long. The pulse wavers in and out of touch. It won't be long.

. . . But this man will not die! The skeleton rouses

173

from its stupor. The snout twitches as if to fend off a fly. What is it that shakes him like a gourd full of beans? The pulse returns, melts away, comes back again, and stays. The respirations are twelve, then fourteen. I have not done it. I did not murder him. I am innocent!

... The man in the bed swallows. His Adam's apple bobs slowly. It would be so easy to do it. Three minutes of pressure on his larynx. He is still not conscious, wouldn't feel it, wouldn't know. My thumb and finger-tips hover, land on his windpipe. My pulse beating in his neck, his in mine. I look back over my shoulder. No one. Two bare IV poles in a corner, their looped metal eyes witnessing. Do it! Fingers press. Again he swallows. Look back again. How closed the door is. And ... my hand wilts. I cannot. It is not in me to do it. Not that way. The man's head swivels like an upturned fish. The squadron of ribs battles on.

... In the corridor the women lean against the wall, against each other. They are like a band of angels dispatched here to take possession of his body. It is the only thing that will satisfy them.

"He didn't die," I say. "He won't, or can't." They are silent.

"He isn't ready yet," I say.

"He *is* ready," the old woman says. "*You* ain't."

Death in the family. A sorrowful passage, sometimes for those left here, alive but grieving, the death of someone we love is an unending wound to the heart. How

174

much worse it is made by public or legal battles surrounding its circumstance.

We do not yet have the laws or the norms in place that permit a person a range of death choices that do not also implicate another person (a doctor or a loved one) in an illegal act. Many advocates for the right to die insist that what is wrong with our society is that the chronically, terminally, and hopelessly ill and their families have so few options for care and maintenance.

As a culture we abhor the notion and the reality of murder. When individuals cannot speak for themselves, and someone else decides that their time is appropriately over, we are burdened with the fear that this is murder. We must find a new way to look at intervention in these matters that makes us both morally responsible and at the same time free of the fear and the label of "murderer." Can we, as a society, redefine these actions to include a rather specific policy of what I like to call "last rights" so that murder or killing are no longer the meaningful or correct labels?

A Doctor Deals Death:
Dr. Kevorkian's Suicide Machine

Dr. Jack Kevorkian is a man with some very controversial ideas; indeed, from his earliest days as a medical student he has been a part of controversy because of his outspoken views. Presumably he ran into difficulties during his student days for a proposal that death row

175

prisoners be rendered unconscious so that medical experimentation could be conducted on them. Kevorkian holds some similar medical ideas to this day. Notions that are, at best, disagreeable, and at worst, terrible curtailments on the rights of prisoners.

Kevorkian's current fame, however, is about another right; he has taken on the issue of the right to die. He has been described by some as a hero, and by others simply as "Dr. Death." Kevorkian actually invented a "suicide machine" that could be operated by the individual wishing to die, once someone else has inserted an intravenous tube into the person's arm. The patient choosing death then pushes a button which causes a painless death in 6 to 10 minutes.

Most of America became aware of Kevorkian in the early summer of 1990 when a woman successfully used the Kevorkian machine to die. Dr. Kevorkian resides in Michigan, interestingly, a state whose laws are somewhat confused with regard to the question of whether aiding a suicide is a crime. Mrs. Janet Adkins lived in Portland, Oregon, and had heard of Dr. Kevorkian when his suicide machine got press attention in the fall of 1989. Suffering from the preliminary stages of Alzheimer's disease and already at the stage where simple tasks were difficult, she contacted Kevorkian, and travelled from Oregon to Michigan to willingly meet her death.

After one meeting, over dinner, Mr. and Mrs. Adkins, a friend of theirs, and Kevorkian all apparently agreed that she was an acceptable candidate for death facilitated by his device. What followed will undoubtedly become part of the American lore about dying. Kevorkian and Adkins went to a public park in a van he had equipped, and plugged the suicide machine into an electrical outlet intended for trailers using the facilities. She was dead within minutes.

The legal and ethical aftermath will prevail long after Adkins' death. It is as yet unclear what the state of Michigan will do about this case and how they will proceed with Dr. Kevorkian. The ethical community is largely unsympathetic to Kevorkian's manner, ideology, and techniques; yet they understand too well the dilemma he dramatically highlights.

A doctor dealing death so openly, almost proudly, against the conventions and the mores of his discipline, is not an easy or a comforting event to observe. Yet, what Dr. Jack "Death" Kevorkian does is to force, by an almost violent confrontation, the issue of how few choices are readily available to those like Mrs. Adkins and others who find themselves in unbearable straits, and who want to choose death.

Complicating Circumstances

As medicine has become so specialized, fewer Americans have personal relationships with their doctors. The family doctor is less and less a reality, and the strong likelihood is that the doctor who treats you in your dying days is not the doctor who was with you through your younger or more vibrant days. More and more of the elderly choose to live in communities geared for their needs; there the doctors are only the doctors of one's old age.

Morris Abram, a distinguished lawyer, who was the chairman of the first Presidential Commission for the Study of Ethical Problems in Medicine and Biomedical and Behavioral Research, said the following about our changing medical landscape:

> Most importantly, there was a relationship that arose with doctors.... They knew their patients and their patients knew them....
>
> ... Treatments occurred in the home. I never knew a death to occur in a hospital in my home town; I never knew a birth to occur in the hospital in my home town. There were no relays of interns who came in and looked at a piece of paper to see what was there, placed before them by someone they didn't even know. There were no weekends off or thirty-day vacations in which new doctors and new teams came in. People were treated *personally*, usually by one physician.
>
> You go to the best hospitals today, as indeed I have spent a lot of time in some, and you cannot recognize the changing cast. They come so fast and furious from so many disciplines, on eight hour shifts and five days a week, each with his own purpose and his own speciality. (Journal of Family Law, *vol. 23 #2, 1985, pp 173-198. "Privacy in the Medical Context")*

Our original notion of the doctor as a part of our extended family is now a part of historical tradition. Now, state legislatures, not family doctors, deal with the questions of dying. And more elected officials note the need for legislation in the area of death and dying; more states have enacted living-will statutes or adopted Quinlan-style laws. Even William Webster, the attorney general of Missouri, who filed the brief against the Cruzans in the supreme court, has endorsed a piece of legislation that would give relief to families like the Cruzans.

It is not the concentration of specialized medicine nor our geographic mobility alone, however, that so confounds privacy rights in the medical domain. With the spectre of the right-to-life suits filed by strangers against both the doctor and the families involved, doctors have even more to worry about than their already burdensome fears of malpractice suits and their difficult task of reconciling a patient's wishes with their own ethical standards.

What could cripple a doctor's humanitarian impulse more quickly than the dread that the sanctity-of-life squads will sue you and drag you through the newspapers and endless court battles for your attempt to help a patient die? Equally worrisome is the possibility that families might give up hope for a relative before they should, for fear of being trapped forever, unable to change their original treatment directives. If Nancy Cruzan's parents had known that they would not be able to order the machines and feeding tubes disconnected after their hope for her had vanished, without appealing to the Supreme Court of the United States, perhaps they would not have elected initially to agree to the life-support measures.

This is not a judgment, or even a speculation, regarding the possible actions or feelings of the Cruzans. It simply illustrates the point. Unless families feel they have autonomy in these life and death matters, it is conceivable that families will begin to be reluctant about employing technological devices, even when the result might be beneficial, if they perceive that their decision is a permanent one.

Toward a Code of Last Passages

We do not want to acknowledge that death is our unavoidable rite of passage, and that as such it demands and requires our attention and our conscious planning. A friend tells the following story. In his twenties, he attended synagogue fairly regularly and remembered the rabbi during each year's Yom Kippur service uttering the following: "Birth is our beginning, and life a journey, a coming, a going.... But *death* ... *death is our destination.*"

This sentence was always delivered with great solemnity and the appropriate dramatic pauses and oratorical flourishes. He angered many members of the congregation and was made fun of by many others because of that simple, if overdramatic and flowery, favorite stock phrase of his.

At the same time in the service each year, my friend's mother would cover part of her face and look sideways at her children, and say: "O god, here he goes again with his death and the destination schtick. Why won't he leave it alone?" Everyone then would all get the uncontrollable giggles, having known ahead of time what was coming from the Rabbi and what would undoubtedly immediately thereafter come from their mother's lips. Secretly, they shared her feelings but knew that they could not possibly get away with the same remark, watched as they were by the stern and patriarchal eye of their father, who demanded complete obedience in shul but who, they had reason to know, had spoken privately to the Rabbi some years before in his own futile attempt to get the Rabbi to cut out his "death and the destination schtick."

In the days before the possibility of respirator-life, and the chance of being sustained in an almost eternal and suspended vegetative state, my own mother was interested in making simpler plans. She wanted to get the burial arrangements made for my father and herself— that is, the fairly straightforward task of purchasing burial plots in the appropriate cemetery. My childhood memories of overheard conversations point poignantly to a much less complicated time. My parents were quite young then. They must have been in their fifties, yet my mother was eager to have this matter resolved.

Perhaps because she had seen so much death in her own family, she had an added sense of urgency. Seeing the face of death so often, maybe she knew better than to deny its existence. I have always felt that her firsthand knowledge of death, from her earliest years, has somehow made her less frightened of it. My father, on the other hand, would have none of it. When the subject of burial would come up, he would say, "You know my desire, bury me on any corner of Times Square, but be sure to pipe in jazz music twenty-four hours a day." Then, as now, discussions of death or dying are met with an outrageous joke or the plea "Please, don't get grisly."

On a recent trip to visit me in New York, on our way to the theater, my father remarked that Times Square had gotten so seedy that maybe he would have to change his mind about his final residence. He then gave that death-defying gesture of his, so familiar to me, a warm, long, loud, laugh with an open mouth and head tilted slightly back, and a flashing twinkle from his ever-vibrant eyes. Even now, at nearly eighty, he cannot take the approach of death to heart. He cannot have a conversation about it, not even about burial, much less a discussion about his wishes given the reality of death in this era. He symbolizes so much about how many of us feel.

Is it superstition? If we talk about how we want to die, might we bring it on? Or speed it up? Andrew Malcolm, describing his own conflicts surrounding the death of his mother, reminds us of our cultural aversion to recognition and planning:

> Doctors know as well as anyone what happens in families when, perhaps over Sunday dinner, an elderly grandmother, comfortable with her own approaching mortality, starts to speak: "Someday when I'm gone ... "
>
> But she is instantly cut off by a chorus of younger voices. "O Grams," they say, "you're going to outlive us all."
>
> The conversation is diverted. No guidance is passed.

And the children, silently watching from behind their mashed potatoes, get the message about what should never be mentioned. ("The Ultimate Decision," Dec. 3, 1989. *New York Times Magazine,* adapted from *Someday.*)

Somewhere deep inside all of us, however, we do understand. At least in a very quiet, private part of ourselves we know that, all the oat bran and alfalfa sprouts notwithstanding, we will die, and so will everyone we cherish. Yet death is viewed as a special kind of failure by remaining family members, and certainly by our doctors.

I'm not sure I know when dying became such a public enterprise. Perhaps the Vietnam War contributed to our inoculation against both the horror and the expectation of privacy in death. Night after night, over our dinner or our cocktails, we watched the war, or so it seemed. Later we would see the results of our use of napalm when we saw the pictures of its victims.

Local television news broadcasts, usually those airing at 10 or 11 P.M. are noted for their graphic reportage of the day's more brutal events. If you watch the late-airing local news in New York City, for example, it is not uncommon to see blood-spattered cars, mangled bodies, and corpses, covered and uncovered. While images have desensitized us and hardened our eyes, this era of publicized death still has not moved us enough to face candidly the personal dimensions of death.

The Museum of Modern Art in New York held an

enormous Andy Warhol retrospective following his untimely death. Rooms were filled with the pop artist/cult figure's famous works—the Campbell soup can, the Marilyn Monroe sequence, the Jackie Kennedy pictures, and many more that have become a part of our popular art, trademarks of the artist and our time.

But the pictures that jumped out at me and that I still see vividly in my mind were his grotesque "photo images" of a fatal car accident. There, in Warhol style, sequential shot after shot, the viewer could virtually experience the accident anew, almost as a firsthand observer. There you could see, up close and in complete detail, someone being decapitated.

When it comes to exposure, disclosure, revelation, and reportage, we, as a society, have definitely lost our innocence. We have developed an eye for the grotesque, the atrocity, the tragedy. We have become quite brave and bloody in our images.

We can face death up close and unafraid, as long as it is a form of media death, and someone else's at that. Paradoxically, we want to hold on tightly to a terribly innocent, mythical, nineteenth-century notion that death is, after all, an inherently private matter and that we don't really need to make any serious plans surrounding it, someone else will take care of those dirty little details for us.

In the right to die, more than in the other domains of privacy, we must declare ourselves, "go on record," as it were, in order to activate this special form of privacy. If

right to die

we are to reach a time when the right to die will be understood as part of our privacy guarantees, we need, as a society, to come to an understanding about the need for our own individual involvement in our deaths. Keeping our families out of court and off the front pages of newspapers, and lessening, to some extent the sorrow we leave in the wake of our departure, require planning and a commitment to the individual's ultimate right in these matters.

That living will that so many believe will be the answer to our problems, even as it is being approved as a valid document or concept in a number of states, is still not prepared by most of us. The privacy one should expect in one's reproductive decisions and one's sexual choices is not so easily replicated in one's dying. We have seen so many times that the right of privacy, inside the family sphere, while recognized as a solid legal precedent, is not always operative in particular cases.

In actuality, "living will" is a false phrase, for it is a "natural death document." For those who would like to preserve the sanctity both of life *and of death*, and who believe that there is still at least the possibility of creating a perfect privacy, the thought of nasty negotiations surrounding one's demise are not at all appealing.

Perhaps, as a nation, we should take a first step at removing, if not the sting of death, at least the sting of its possible attendant horrors, by training and providing "natural death counselors" who could aid in our discussing death, as well as help, in a standard and routine way, preparation of the appropriate documentation. The question of how to die and who can or should take responsibility might better be handled by professionals outside the family, the formal legal arena, and the medical profession—professionals trained especially to help us understand our options, as well as the range of things that might occur, while we are still healthy, lucid, and far from the time when our desires will need to be enforced.

Death is a rite of passage. Until we can accept it, and embrace it as such, natural death will continue to be a random occurrence for those of us lucky enough to have that fate. Perhaps it will be a long time before the right to die will be an easy or automatically guaranteed, universal right, because such fundamental ethical dilemmas are raised.

These are conflicts and dilemmas that have been at the heart of moral, philosophical, and theological debates since the beginning of human history. Yet a democratic society, while honoring the validity of these diverse claims about life and death, must not turn away from those areas of personal liberty that stimulate profound and troublesome debate and controversy. The claim that we ought to be entitled to a series of "last rights" is not made less legitimate, or less viable, simply because it raises such complex and thorny issues.

The Paradoxes of
Intimacy: A Postscript

The vast array of choices in reproduction, in kinds of sexual love, in ways of dying—these are the most private questions of our lives, yet they represent the issues of our public and our political battles.

We have become a public, publicized, and politicized society, but the politicization of privacy has not served us uniformly well. The politics of privacy has become a dialogue between age-old and antagonistic ideologies— namely, the conflict between the belief in the inherent worth and good of personal and individual freedom versus the belief in regulation and control of other's lives for the presumed public good.

When privacy is part of the conversation of "rights," it is segregated into the domain of civil liberties, where freedoms have almost always been won through struggle, surrounded by strife. In the personal business of privacy, this struggle has become less a noble enterprise and more a bitter and ideological tug-of-war.

Unborn life versus fully formed female life; traditional and moralistic approaches to sexuality versus open and joyous homosexuality; personal choice in matters of death and dying versus religious or legal mandates. Is this the material for an ennobling debate about the meaning of rights in a civilized society, or is it instead the stuff of bitter ideological warfare?

Increasingly, voters make election decisions based on the single issue of abortion, and candidates see the abortion issue as a deciding factor in their fates. While it is encouraging to see previously ambivalent or even hostile candidates change from anti-choice to a pro-choice stance, something in it is profoundly sad.

Decisions about the competence of those who govern the rest of us should not be reduced to their views on what goes on inside the private realm of a woman's womb, nor should candidates be able to get by with campaigns based solely or primarily on their views about choice in reproduction.

In the last two decades we have had an unprecedented explosion of claims, of rights, of liberties. Never before in our history have we been asked to contend with so many open, public, and divergent lifestyles and life choices. As some of us have claimed more autonomy and less conformity in our lives, others of us have come to believe that so much unfettered nonconformity and autonomy in personal life decisions is too much, is damaging the body politic, and ought to be controlled. This expansion of choices in our intimate worlds has led some to feel justified not only in their negative feelings but also in their actions to try to force the nation into conformity in lifestyle and choice.

Increasing the available choices about reproduction, sexual style, and dying also increases tensions as we are inevitably confronted with people who are doing things we do not like, find morally reprehensible, or even worse. In these most intimate areas the field is ripe for censure, because these are dilemmas some believe must be reserved for ultimate arbitration by a highly personal definition of God and good.

We cannot, however, become the keepers of our neighbor's morals nor the judges of their lives. Dangerous and difficult as it sometimes is, within certain guidelines, individuals should be trusted with the personal morality of their own lives, even if their choices would not, or could not, be our own. It is a deeply acknowledged part of the American tradition that freedom brings with it a set of perplexing and troubling questions and the stark reality that not all among us will exercise good judgment in their private decisions nor that everyone will seek the common good. The dilemma has been captured by Ronald Dworkin when he says: "It is an old problem for liberal theory, how far people should have the right to do the wrong thing. . . . " Yet individual choices must remain just that, and a lost code of honor about the sanctity of individual choice and action should be restored. The control of the private lives of the evil few would undoubtedly bring with it severe restrictions and abuses for the overwhelming majority of good people whose private actions do not need to be monitored for dangerous or hurtful intent.

Perhaps the case-by-case approach to privacy that we have developed confounds rather than clarifies privacy. We need instead to develop a broad-based and normative understanding of privacy rather than a restricted and political policy of privacy.

Intimacy itself is all too often so vulnerable and fragile; it is not a creature of the streets and the courts. Warfare in these most intimate worlds has done the greatest harm to the most vulnerable among us. Vulnerability and privacy are not compatible partners, as I trust I have shown. We must think about the goal of an "equality of vulnerability." Being rendered very vulnerable ought not be determined primarily by one's race, gender, sexual orientation, age, or income group, as it now increasingly appears to be. Currently we are entrapped in a kind of "regulated" privacy, encoded by law and upheld or dismissed by the courts. This cannot produce an equality of privacy, nor will it equalize vulnerability. Instead it reinforces the disturbing notion that privacy rights are easily obtained only if you are lucky enough to be well placed in the system or fortunate enough to share the views of the prevailing majority.

Index